FLYING
FEATHERS

Iain Grahame

Foreword by
Gerald Durrell

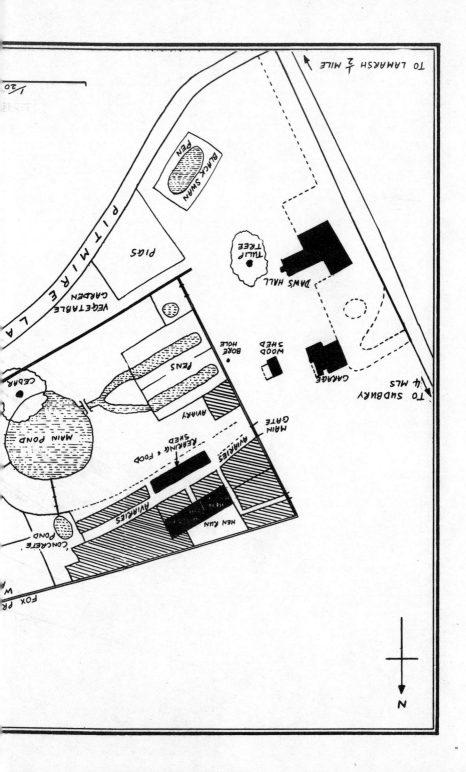

Also by Iain Grahame

Jambo Effendi
Blood Pheasant

Flying Feathers

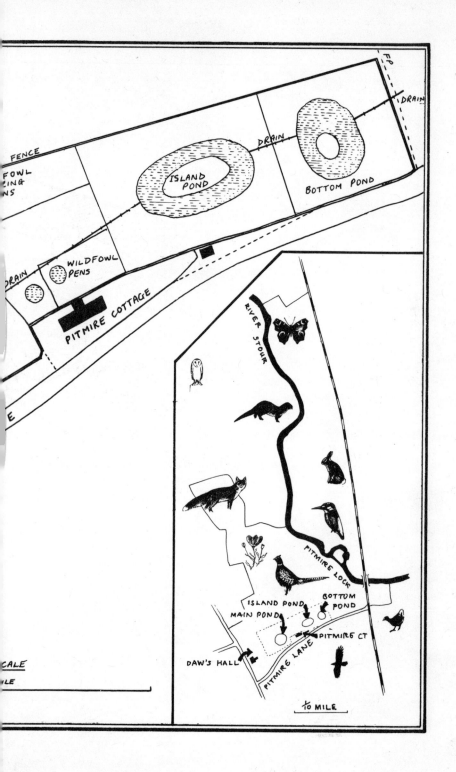

ISLAND POND

DRAIN

BOTTOM POND

FENCE

FOWL
ZING
NS

DRAIN

FP

DRAIN

WILDFOWL
PENS

PITMIRE COTTAGE

RIVER STOUR

PITMIRE LOCK

ISLAND POND

BOTTOM POND

MAIN POND

PITMIRE CT

DAW'S HALL

PITMIRE LANE

½ MILE

SCALE

½ MILE

FLYING FEATHERS

IAIN GRAHAME

Foreword by Gerald Durrell

Illustrations by Timothy Greenwood

ST. MARTIN'S PRESS
NEW YORK

Foreword

This is a book written by an enthusiast.

There have been hundreds of books written by enthusiasts, and I have been bored by so many of them that I must hastily qualify my opening statement by saying that this is a well-written and humorous book by an enthusiast.

Iain Grahame is a lucky man, for he has not only achieved what he has set out to do — a boast few of us can make — but he is also able to write about it and thus to share his pleasures with others. He writes with a nice sense of the ridiculous and an infectious humour, which adds enormous charm to his story of Daw's Hall, with its varied collection of carefully observed and carefully nurtured creatures, ranging from pot-bellied pigs to pheasants.

But there is much more to Daw's Hall than simply a collection of charming animals. There is a serious conservation motive. Both the ducks and the pheasants upon which Iain Grahame concentrates are under great pressure in the wild state, and many are in danger of extinction, for they are good to eat, and their habitats dwindle as the forests are felled and the marshland and lakes are drained. If nothing else, Daw's Hall has made a major contribution to captive breeding — a new form of conservation which is, each year, gaining in importance. The establishment of the blood pheasants outlined in this book is, in itself, a major avicultural and conservation achievement, and one that proves Daw's Hall to be not just simply a back-yard zoo but an establishment with a purpose. Would that there were many more like it.

If my daily post bag is anything to go by, three-quarters of the population of the United Kingdom wants to do exactly what Iain

Grahame has successfully done, for everywhere there lurk people who long to complicate their lives by closer association with parrots and polar bears, chimpanzees and cacomistles, ravens and rhinos. Britain seems to be a nation of frustrated zoo owners. In future, when they write to me for advice, I shall have great pleasure in recommending this gay and informative book to them, as I now do to you.

Gerald Durrell

Introduction

'What on earth made you think of setting up a wildfowl farm?' is a question that I am often asked by people who visit our strange menagerie. The short and honest answer is that, when I retired from the Army in 1963, I was prepared to do almost anything reasonably legal to avoid having to spend my working hours on a crowded commuter train or in some stuffy office in London. Farming was my first choice, and I enrolled at an agricultural college and for one year I became a short-haired, antediluvian student. Bird-watching and the study of nature had always been a hobby, but at that time I had no idea that such things as wildfowl farms even existed. Then, one day, I happened to drive past a signboard advertising the presence of just such an establishment. Half an hour's talk with the owner convinced me that this was the life for me.

So, Daw's Hall Wildfowl Farm came into being more by accident than by design. I had never even kept a budgerigar or canary as a child, and our methods at first were distinctly amateurish. The arrival, as farm manager, of a huge bearded Dutchman, standing six foot eight inches tall in his size sixteen gumboots, changed our whole approach quite dramatically. Mainly through his herculean endeavours, the farm has gradually taken shape and all sorts of remarkable and fascinating creatures have taken up residence with us. Though most of the waterfowl and pheasants are confined to the farm, orphaned ducklings do periodically invade the house and pot-bellied pigs from Vietnam have usurped the garage. An enchanting trumpeter bird from South America was at his happiest when hooting loudly from on top of the dining-room table in the middle of a dinner party.

We make no excuse for pandering to the physical and psychological requirements of our birds and animals. Many of them are now rare or endangered in the wild, so their proper treatment in captivity is of the utmost importance. The breeding of most of them is usually straightforward, but there are some birds that tax our ingenuity to the limit. The Himalayan blood pheasant, for example, had never been successfully kept or bred in captivity anywhere in the world outside its natural habitat until we were fortunate enough to raise them in 1972.

We have certainly learned over the past thirteen years how many gaps there are in our knowledge, and our few successes have been punctuated with frequent moments of horror and hilarity. But above all, it has been and continues to be a happy and rewarding life. For this we are eternally grateful to all the strange creatures that appear in this book, to whom we owe our good fortune.

Iain Grahame
Daw's Hall
1977

Chapter One

Memories of earliest childhood are often frustratingly incomplete. Those events that stand four-square against the passing years, though few in number and seemingly trivial at the time, often execise considerable influence on us in later years.

This was certainly true of my mother's total aversion towards zoos and circuses, which she believed to be invariably cruel. Ill-treatment of any living creature was something that amounted to an obsession with her. Flowers in a vase without water affected her almost as deeply as a lion or tiger pacing endlessly up and down the narrow confines of its cage. Horse-drawn carts were a common sight on the roads in England in those days, and I shall never forget the startled look on the face of the local dustman when she drew alongside him in the Bentley and gave him a broadside for keeping an obviously undernourished animal.

For my fifth birthday my mother gave me a goldfish. Goldie was installed in a spacious glass tank on the nursery table and pebbles, plants and every other possible luxury were added for his comfort. It was my very first pet, and we used to gaze open-mouthed at one another for hours on end with wonder and boredom respectively. Our relationship, however, was destined to be abruptly shattered. One day, when Nanny was off, I was re-enacting across the furniture Wolfe's heroic scaling of the Heights of Quebec. Nearing the summit of the ironing-board, my tiny fingers lost their hold and in falling I clutched at my precious goldfish's abode. Together we hurtled to the floor where, to my undying shame, I watched helplessly as poor Goldie flapped briefly and expired. My mother, hearing the commotion, rushed upstairs. Soaked clothes and cut knees were totally ignored as all her attention was focused on the

1

pathetic piscine remains. Goldie in death was to her no less glorious than Goldie swimming lugubriously round his tank. Reverently he was laid to rest in a little grave beneath my bedroom window, while I was banished, wet, bleeding and miserable, to my room for the rest of the day.

For a long time my sister and I were not allowed to go to any zoo or circus. The nearest we ever came to one was when we had a fleeting glimpse of Regent's Park Zoo from the top of a double-decker bus. Its very name came to have gremlin-like connotations. Then one day — I must have been about six at the time and my sister three — our mother relented, or so it seemed. It transpired that she had decided the time was ripe to give us a personally conducted tour of the accursed precincts. Chessington Zoo, only a short distance from where we lived in Surrey, was selected. Apart from having a ride on a pony (which I fell off) and a Big Dipper (on which I was sick), I can remember nothing of what we saw nor of what my mother said that day. Sadly, I was never able to ask her, for she was killed during an air-raid the following year. That the visit made a profound and lasting impression on me is unquestionable, for more than twenty years elapsed before I visited another zoo. I have never been to the circus and never shall. When my own children sit rapturously enjoying the circus on television, I can share with them the laughter and excitement of clowns and acrobats. When performing lions and elephants come into the arena, I prefer to look away.

All this may sound trite, particularly from someone who to all intents and purposes now has a zoo of his own. I do feel, however, that, paradoxically, my early upbringing has helped me to choose a way of life that I shall never regret. It has certainly been responsible for my firm philosophy that, when man takes it upon himself (whether through motives of pleasure, profit or conservation) to keep any creature in captivity, only one standard of treatment is acceptable. That my mother saw fit to drum home this message into my obtuse little head at a very early age I shall be forever grateful.

As a child, I used to get extremely bored being endlessly asked what I wanted to do when I grew up. Apart from the alternatives of tinker, tailor, etc. that my prune stones disclosed, my future seemed, to me at any rate, reasonably clear from an early age. Since I had no wish to be killed in battle, I knew that the one thing I wasn't going to become was a soldier. Having flirted briefly with the possibilities of missionary and guinea-pig keeper, I settled firmly for farmer.

In fact, I became a soldier for thirteen years and enjoyed every moment. The only campaign I took part in was against the Mau Mau in Kenya. Since their armoury was in the main confined to *pangas* and bows and arrows, and since we always seemed to outnumber the enemy by at least ten to one *and* got a glittering medal for our bravery at the end, it was a rewarding experience for a young man not yet twenty-one. I remained, seconded from my own regiment to the King's African Rifles, for seven happy years. My battalion was based at the headwaters of the Nile, at Jinja in Uganda, and comprised roughly thirty British officers and NCO's and about seven hundred large and lovable *askari*, mainly from the warrior tribes in the North. There was one particular moon-faced giant of a lance corporal whom I got to know very well. Though almost totally illiterate at the time, he was one of the most outstanding natural leaders of men that I have ever met. His name was Idi-son-of-Amin.

What influenced and fascinated me most during my time in East Africa was the wildlife, particularly the birds. There were about fifteen hundred different varieties to be seen, and every type of habitat, from the snow-covered peaks to the steaming tropical forests, had its own gems of the avian kingdom. Jinja, lying almost on top of the Equator, was a wonderful base from which to visit every possible place of interest within the three territories. I seized every opportunity I could, often driving through the night, to enable me to spend longer periods in far-off places. Westward lay the Queen Elizabeth National Park, flanked by the legendary Mountains of the Moon.

Although Ptolemy's *Map of the World* (c. 150 AD) plots with surprising accuracy these selfsame *Lunae Montes* as the birthplace of the Nile, no less than seventeen hundred years elapsed before a white man set foot in Uganda and the true source of the Nile was discovered. Close to our barracks a rock marked the spot from which, in 1862, John Hanning Speke had his first glimpse of the mighty river thundering out of Lake Victoria over what he christened the Ripon Falls. In the context of recent events in Uganda, it is salutary to remember the remarkably short period of European influence and involvement in the country. Its history

3

prior to the latter half of the last century has been likened by one authority to 'a crime to which there have been no eye-witnesses'. Events a hundred years later were not dissimilar and it is, I think, appropriate to mention that I myself wrote at a time when, outwardly at least, law and order prevailed, that 'experience was beginning to prove that civilizing influences often merely delayed, rather than prevented, a reversion to barbarism and anarchy.'*

Murchison Falls Park, about two hundred miles to the north of Jinja, was another Mecca of wildlife. There, where the Nile dramatically narrowed to a gap of only twenty feet before plunging chaotically over a steep abyss, were to be found reminders of the huge herds of game that abounded before the Arabs and white men introduced firearms. The birds, too, were legion. All along the river could be seen kingfishers, storks, egrets, lily-trotters and the dazzlingly beautiful bee-eaters that nested in the sandy river banks. Away from the water, the huge and ungainly ground hornbill and the aptly-named secretary bird (both of which feed on snakes) contrasted with the tiny flashes of gold, amethyst and scarlet that were sunbirds. One of the commonest sounds was the screaming call of the fish eagle, the most nostalgic noise that I know. I heard this same eerie cry after I left East Africa and returned to England. It was the occasion of my first visit to a zoo since Chessington and it made me understand a little better how my mother felt about wild creatures in captivity.

1962 was for me a time for decision. I had recently married and Uganda had just achieved independence. My current tour with the King's African Rifles was finished and my wife, d'Esterre, and I returned home on leave, knowing that a further tour of service with the KAR was unlikely to be allowed. A crash programme had started in 1961 to train African officers, NCO's and technicians to take over from us. It was an operation that, for reasons of political expediency, mass national hysteria in Uganda and appalling ignorance at home, leapt into overdrive without ever engaging any lower gear. As such it was doomed to end in disaster. We both felt that it was, very sadly, a time for 'fresh fields and pastures new.'

There was a period, shortly after the last war, when advertisements in the personal columns of *The Times*, headed 'Retired officer seeks employment' and 'Gentleman, early thirties,

Jambo Effendi, 1966

4

no particular qualifications etc.', opened up a Pandora's box of remunerative careers. Tip-top companies and firms vied with one another for the privilege of offering a seat on the board to recently retired brigadiers, air commodores, naval captains and scions of eminent public schools. The only response to my ten guinea advertisement was an offer to sell life insurance in Peckham. I had arrived too late on the scene. Undaunted, I plumped for my childhood choice of farmer. The only difficulty, as d'Esterre pointed out, was that I had precious little knowledge of the subject and even less capital on which to embark.

The entry form which I received from the bursar of the Royal Agricultural College at Cirencester was somewhat disconcerting. Parents were obliged to sign a certificate confirming that their sons had passed a horrifyingly large number of 'O' levels. Not only had I no parents but, worse still, 'O' levels had yet to be introduced when I attended my particular *alma mater*. When I entered my little white lies on the form and posted it back (duly signed with an illegible, left-handed scrawl with the help of a borrowed pen) the years fell off my shoulders. D'Esterre cut almost a foot off the legs of my colonial-style military shorts remarking, 'I'm sure, if you practise, you'll make the 2nd Eleven at soccer,' and busied herself over suitable provisions for my tuck-box. For my part, I grudgingly agreed to give up smoking cigars and bought a tube of ointment that promised to prevent athlete's foot.

The only thing that slightly marred the jollity of the occasion was that I had to pay my own school fees in advance. For this reason, I felt bound to pay full attention to my studies. 'Gosh, Uncle,' my fellow pupils would say. 'Surely you're not going to bother about old Sweaty's Animal Husbandry lecture tomorrow. *We're* all going to the Cheltenham Gold Cup.' And off they would go in their Donegal tweeds and fast cars, leaving the 'swats' and '*Dad's Army*' to listen to old Sweaty holding forth on the lactation periods of the Friesian cow. The epithet of 'Uncle' jarred a little at first, but it hurt less when two other fellow-sufferers were respectively christened Fossil and Methuselah. 'Uncle', moreover, created quite a stir when he got into the final of the College squash competition and was only beaten by a county player fifteen years his junior. The squash matches which we played against other schools were always a bit of a lark. When they were over, we used to repair to a local pub, where we consumed a lot of beer, told dirty stories and sang bawdy ballads.

As my year's course drew to a close I became aware of two things. The first was that, with the price of land having recently soared to astronomic heights, the number of acres that my limited capital would buy hardly made for a viable agricultural unit. Secondly, I was growing increasingly disillusioned by 'Comparative Gross Outputs of Livestock per acre', 'Receipt Profiles', the 'Gross Margin Analysis System' and similar verbiage that was constantly being thrust down our throats. Although lip service was paid during our course to the dangers of saturating Mother Earth with chemical fertilisers and pesticides, one was left in no doubt that the only acceptable yardstick of modern farming was economic viability by any means within the law. The current vogue for ripping up hedgerows, burning stubble and squirting from an aeroplane solutions of N_{13} P_2O5_{13} K_2O_{20} (a general-purpose fertiliser, to the uninitiated) pointed to a very different form of farming to that which I had envisaged. I detested also the new, effeminate terminology. At College I never once heard the word muck, its successor was farmyard manure, invariably abbreviated to FYM.

From the age of eight to eighteen my holidays had been spent on a delightful, old-fashioned, and doubtless unprofitable, farm in East Suffolk, where I had rejoiced in the open air, the freedom and the song of the birds. There I had served my apprenticeship by topping mangle-wurzels for the cattle, carrying snares and ferret-box for the gamekeeper, learning how to harness and work the old carthorses and a host of other jobs. At first, I despaired of ever being able to handle the Suffolk Punches, until one day old Robinson, the farm bailiff, took me on one side. The gist of his message, conveyed in a rich and fruity dialect liberally punctuated with Anglo-Saxon expletives, was that the hosses were having a bit of difficulty in interpreting my falsetto Oxford accent. Casting my inhibitions aside, I started again, and, much to the amusement of the stockmen, the animals were soon responding to my 'wodi', 'cuppi-wi' and 'ho'd up thar you o'd Davil'. Hard by the horse pond lay the pigsties, where old Bawldrey (who never used anything but his teeth to castrate the piglets) grunted and wallowed with his large whites. Harvest time and all that went with it was not merely a tradition and the climax to the farming year; it was a time for team-work and good fellowship, with every

6

As a child I carried snares and the ferret-box for the gamekeeper.

able-bodied man, woman and child doing their bit to help. The
part we youngsters enjoyed most was when the binder had reduced
the area of standing corn to the last acre, for it was then that the
rabbits started to bolt. Knocking them over with a stick on the run
as they dodged in and out of the stooks was no mean art. Sometimes
a terrified creature would dart under a fallen sheaf and the nearest
lad would, with screams of encouragement from the rest of us, hurl
himself bodily onto it. Nowadays, on many farms the harvest
seems such a clinical and soulless operation. All day long the
combine harvesters churn their way inexorably across the desolate
acres, and in the evenings the drivers repair from the charred
battlefields to the equally smoky pubs and bingo halls.

It was during the harvest of 1963 that, with thoughts such as
these running through my mind, I drove up from Cirencester to

view a farm that had recently come up for sale in Suffolk. By this time I was pretty well convinced that if we were going to farm at all, then the acreage had got to be small and the enterprise unconventional. The whole gamut of agricultural crops, from the exotic sounding Elite Lepeuple wheat and Sharpe's Klein Polybeet to Warwick 277 and Wisconsin 273 (these latter sounding far more suitable for dialling on the telephone than for actually growing in a field), left me horribly cold. No! It had got to be livestock. But what? D'Esterre, who had loyally and uncomplainingly put up with all my crazy notions, was, just as flummoxed as I was over exactly what particular creature or creatures we should keep.

The farm that I went to view turned out to be grossly over-priced and there was planning permission for a housing estate just across the boundary. My route home took me through a village in West Suffolk where, as I slowed down to cross a bridge, I saw some beautiful ducks paddling contentedly in the river below. I knew enough to realise that these were no ordinary farmyard ducks, nor were they mallard, tufted, pintail or any of the commoner British birds. Looking more carefully I saw to my amazement that among them was a pair of Hottentot teal, birds that I had often seen, and shot, in East Africa. I noticed beside the road a smartly painted sign which read 'Priory Waterfowl Farm'. The last word intrigued me, and I decided to investigate. All sorts of outlandish possibilities were already racing through my mind as I drove into a small courtyard and parked the car.

I found the owner perched on an upturned bucket, plucking gorgeous feathers from the rear end of a loudly protesting peacock. There are some people whose professions, past or present, stand out like the proverbial sore thumb, and this man, with the neatly clipped moustache and cavalry twill trousers, was no exception. 'Yes?' he barked in the same staccato voice as he had doubtless used when demanding 'Number, rank and name?' in more virile years. Only just restraining myself from leaping smartly to attention and saluting, I doffed my cap and introduced myself. This was clearly not enough, so involuntarily I stammered something about having recently bought a property containing a large lake, I was looking for some suitable waterfowl with which to stock it. 'And a few peafowl might look nice on the lawn,' I added as an afterthought. The Colonel's manner visibly thawed and, rising to his feet, he invited me to come and inspect his stock. The

8

Plucking feathers from the train of a loudly protesting peacock.

peacock, duly released, raced off to its womenfolk who were, I imagined, somewhat less keen on the short back and sides than their master. He explained, however, that since these birds moulted and lost their beautiful trains every summer he was merely helping nature on its way and avoiding a pile of feathers all over his farm. 'Can't have an untidy cleaning area, can we, old boy?' to which I politely concurred.

It was a lovely sunny day and, as we strolled round his enclosures, I could not but be impressed with his knowledge and enthusiasm. His menagerie consisted of swans, geese, ducks, bantams, peafowl, exotic pheasants, pigeons and a couple of spaniels. The waterfowl, he told me, were classified into two main categories — domestic and ornamental. The former consisted of large and, to me, rather uninteresting birds that were clearly destined for duck à *l'orange* or goose liver *pâté*, while the ornamental breeds comprised a whole range of wild waterfowl distributed around the world. They all looked incredibly lovely, but the Colonel explained that they also moulted annually and were at present in their dull eclipse plumage. I wondered whether they too were subjected to the peacock plucking treatment.

Some of his waterfowl lived in a series of small paddocks, while others had attractively planted enclosures that ran down to the river itself. There were mandarins and Carolinas, pochard and pintail, and large ungainly eiders that waddled out of the water and tried to undo our shoe-laces. A mixed flock of geese — snows, barnacles, emperors and whitefronts — grazed avidly on the short grass, honking and grunting quietly among themselves. All the birds were tame and all looked sleek and contented. The only rather unattractive sight was an eight foot chain-link fence that ran round the perimeter. The Colonel explained to me that, while a three foot fence of wire netting was perfectly adequate to contain pinioned birds, the high fence was necessary to keep out foxes and other unwanted intruders.

I became more and more fascinated by this marvellous collection. There were many questions I wanted to ask, but felt rather inhibited knowing I was there under somewhat false pretences. The Colonel, however, seemed in no apparent hurry and, by merely listening to him, I managed to glean quite a lot about his unusual farm. One aspect that particularly appealed to me was that here at last were some livestock that were not merely regarded as objects on a sheet of graph paper which, to ensure their survival, had to justify the quantity of food forced into their wretched little bellies. Nor, like battery hens or veal calves, were they doomed to an all too brief and unnatural existence. The market and the slaughter-house, which I can never visit without a momentary pang of sadness, were happily avoided and, like breeders of labradors or Shetland ponies, one could, to a certain extent, choose one's customers. Whichever way I looked at it, this extraordinary form of farming, which before that day I had never heard of, seemed to be the answer to all my prayers. By the time we were half way round his collection, I felt like Joan of Arc hearing her voices and could hardly wait to get back to Cirencester and break the joyful news to d'Esterre.

'You're mad,' she said, and then, as if I needed convincing, 'absolutely stark, staring, raving mad.'

I tactfully refrained from opening a bottle of champagne to celebrate, but instead poured out two large whiskies and soda and tried to explain it all to her. After replenishing her glass once and mine at least three times I was still no nearer to persuading her that I did not need psychiatric treatment.

'You really can't expect me to enthuse over your spending the rest of your life carrying a bucket of corn round a few scrawny old ducks,' she said, 'and anyway what on earth makes you think you can make any money out of it?'

I had to admit that here she had a point. Though sorely tempted, I had refrained from asking the Colonel whether I could cast my eye quickly over his profit and loss account, but a few remarks he had casually let slip seemed to imply that trade was brisk.

'He even had a waiting list for some of the really expensive birds,' I mentioned hopefully.

'You really are the most naive man I've ever met,' she said. 'He's probably never even bred them.' 'Anyway,' and I sensed the trump card coming out, 'I thought you disapproved of wild creatures being kept in captivity. The poor little things,' she added cunningly, 'being pinioned, they won't even be able to fly off on migration.'

I made a few lame comments about 'huge planted enclosures' and 'plenty of natural water', but since we were getting nowhere, I said I had a headache and was going to bed. As I climbed unsteadily up the stairs, I heard mutterings of 'hardly surprising after all that whisky,' before she put through a long and extremely expensive telephone call to her mother.

'Mummy says why don't you become a stockbroker?' was an opening gambit that she had tried once before at the breakfast table. We both knew from experience that it was not conducive to marital bliss over the cornflakes. I had spent a sleepless night, churning over the pros and cons in my mind, and I realised that d'Esterre's reactions were perfectly justified. Somehow, I had to find out much more about what an ornamental waterfowl farm entailed and then, if it still seemed a practical proposition, I had to convince her that it was the right thing for us.

'Tell you what,' I said brightly after pretending to scan the newspapers for a few moments. 'Why don't we both go over to Slimbridge for the day?'

'Slimbridge?'

'Yes, you know, Peter Scott's Wildfowl Trust. It can't be more than an hour's drive away. I've been a member for years and I'm sure they will give us some advice.'

'But today's Monday, darling, and I thought you said they were going to teach you how to plough this morning.'

'**** the ploughing!' I replied, 'Uncle is going to play truant today, and anyway. . .isn't the little boutique that you've always wanted to go to on our way?'

By mid-morning we were at Slimbridge and, being a weekday, it was not at all crowded. We found the curator supervising the moving of a family of recently hatched ducklings into their rearing pen. Their foster-mother, a wonderfully docile and patient bantam, was clucking encouragingly over a little bowl of chopped egg, lettuce and all sorts of other succulent morsels. Every so often she would pick up some delectable tidbit and the braver ducklings would jump up and seize it from her beak. Only when they scurried off and jumped headlong into a small bowl of water, did she seem rather perplexed by the strange, aquatic habits of her children.

Tommy Johnstone, the curator, could not have been more helpful. It was also encouraging to both of us that he did not bat an eyelid when we explained that we were thinking of trying to make a living out of keeping and breeding ornamental waterfowl. He took us first of all to the perimeter fence, which was similar to the Colonel's, and explained how to erect it in a way that stops foxes from climbing over or burrowing underneath. Then we looked at his breeding pens, rearing equipment, incubation room and foodshed. Finally, he gave us a copy of the Wildfowl Trust price list of surplus birds and recommended suitable literature for us to read. Needless to say, by the time we left, I was besotted with the fascinating range of exotic waterfowl that we had seen and with the idea of starting up a similar collection. Whether the visit to the boutique on our way home helped, I do not know, but gradually d'Esterre's opposition to the idea faded. The subject of a career in the City was tactfully avoided and it was wonderful to be able to

12

plan the future together.

Back at the College the news spread like wild-fire: 'I say, Uncle, is it true that you're going to keep funny birds?' and 'We'll certainly know where to come for our Christmas dinners!' were just some of the more polite comments to greet me.

After our visit to the Wildfowl Trust there were only a few more weeks left before the end of term and the completion of my year's course. And I must confess to having been thoroughly selective over the lectures that I attended during those weeks. I took copious notes on land drainage, farm accounting and the anatomy and diseases of poultry, and much of my time was spent in poring over ornithological books at home and talking to the local gamekeepers about broody hens and vermin control. Instructions to estate agents in East Anglia, who had been asked to let us know of mixed farms of two to three hundred acres that came up for sale, were dramatically amended, as what we wanted was a period farmhouse, a tenth of the original acreage and, most important of all, a constant supply of spring-fed water.

We soon discovered that definitions of 'spring-fed water' appeared to vary as much as those of 'desirable residences'. More than once we motored vast mileages, only to find plastic goldfish ponds or puddles on the lawn caused by a leaking tap, blocked cesspit or slurry from the pig-sties. Then, one of the Norfolk broads came on the market. It was a heavenly spot, miles from anywhere, and I fell rapturously in love with it. D'Esterre, however, was rather less enthusiastic and pointed out that, although there were no less than one hundred and sixty three acres of glorious reedbeds and water, to say nothing of bearded tits and marsh harriers, there was less than half an acre of dry land. Grudgingly, I agreed that the proportion was a trifle impractical.

One day in the spring of 1964 we had arranged to see three different properties in Suffolk and Essex. The first was in a terrible state of repair, the second was way beyond our means, and our morale was at a low ebb when we approached the third and final house on our list. Although it stood close to a narrow country lane, an avenue of lime trees made it very difficult for us to see much of the house from the road. What little we could see did not impress us. Brown paintwork on the window frames and long grass and nettles were very much in evidence. The estate agent's leaflet had advertised 'sweeping lawns and a small and a large pond'. Peering through the undergrowth, I could just see a pond that measured about ten foot at the widest point. We were then so disillusioned by estate agents' terminology that I was quite prepared to assume that this was the larger of the two advertised. Though there was certainly a small area of nicely mown grass, the 'sweeping lawns' seemed something of a sweeping statement. I was all for leaving the poor owners in peace, but d'Esterre was insistent that having made an appointment we must keep to it.

Daw's Hall, with a cottage and sixteen acres of land, had last changed hands for nine hundred and fifty pounds thirty years previously, when the present owners had bought it for fruit growing on their return from service in India. They were a charming couple and clearly saddened at the thought of having to move in their old age from a place that had become too much for them to maintain.

First, we inspected the house. It was a strange building of constrasting styles. Built some time during the sixteenth century, part of it had been gutted by fire and rebuilt at the beginning of the last century. The oak beams, large fireplaces and low ceilings of the Tudor period contrasted strongly with the spacious proportions of the Georgian era. It exuded a wonderfully happy atmosphere. The land, apart from the garden which was dominated by an enormous tulip tree, consisted of an old apple orchard, two paddocks and a pond. I asked whether we could see the pond first. It was totally surrounded by tall trees and undergrowth and right beside it, in a splendid cedar tree, I heard a lesser-spotted woodpecker, now very rare in many parts of England. The whole tree was pock-marked with woodpecker holes, and blackcaps and other warblers trilled in the bushes. A pair of moorhens scurried across the water at our approach. Although the pond was not particularly large, it was beautiful and peaceful. It must have dated from the time when the clay was dug for the original house, which would have been constructed of daub and wattle. Standing there four hundred years later, with the rays of the afternoon sun forming dancing shadows on the water, I could think of no more perfect setting for our ornamental waterfowl. D'Esterre was equally enthusiastic. Our reverie, however, was suddenly broken by the owner's wife.

'You'd never think that at least three people have drowned in this pond, would you?' she said. 'Two suicides and one murder, if I

14

remember correctly,' she added laconically.

'Gosh!' said d'Esterre. I was too shattered to say anything.

'Oh yes, the woman who was murdered is the one who's supposed to haunt the house now. Hundreds of years ago a couple who lived here had apparently hoarded away a lot of treasure. The word got round and some foreigner — Spanish, I think he was — was determined to steal it and inveigled his way into the household. One night the lady of the house caught him trying to find the treasure and, in a moment of panic, he stabbed her and threw her into this pond.'

'Have you ever seen her?' I asked.

'No, we haven't, but a lot of the locals told us years ago when we bought this place that we must be mad wanting to live in the "haunted house of Lamarsh". I know that many of the older people even now won't go past the house at night. Market day is on Thursdays and there's a bus to take people to Sudbury in the morning and back again in the afternoon. I've heard of people who, having missed the bus and, rather than walk past here down to the village on a winter's evening, have gone miles across the fields on the other side of the river. Anyway,' she laughed, 'I must remember that we're trying to sell the place and I mustn't put you off by a lot of old rubbish about a ghost! I can honestly say that we've always found it a thoroughly happy and unspooky house.'

Ghost or no ghost, I knew instinctively that d'Esterre was already sold on Daw's Hall. I had only one reservation, and that was whether there was sufficient water in the area to make more ponds for the birds. When I put this question to the owner, his wife responded by asking whether I had a pen-knife. Mystified, I dutifully obliged. Striding over to a hazel tree, she cut a Y-shaped piece of wood from one of the branches and announced: 'I'll soon show you how much water there is.' She then led us away from the pond and back to the lawn where we watched, fascinated, as she gave a display of water divining.

'Look,' she said, after walking along slowly for a few yards with the hazel twig held parallel to the ground, 'plenty of water here.' Her face, which had until then registered intense concentration, suddenly changed. The muscles round her mouth tightened and the knuckles on her hands went white, as she strained to keep the divining-stick horizontal. Suddenly, she could bear it no longer and the point of the stick shot down to a vertical position.

15

'How on earth did you learn to do that?' I asked.

'There's nothing difficult about it,' she said. 'An old gardener showed me this method years ago. It's like hypnotism, you've either got it in you or you haven't, and how it works I haven't the faintest idea. Why don't you have a go?'

D'Esterre tried first, walking trance-like around the garden and going several times over the magical spot, but the stick never wavered. Then I tried. To begin with, I succeeded so well in blanking my mind from my surroundings that I tripped over a tree root and fell flat on my face, ramming the hazel stick hard into my ribs. At the second attempt I discarded the nonchalant, Madonna-like approach and, instead, strode purposefully straight to the place where the owner had found water. I was several feet away when I first felt the pull and the nearer I came the stronger it was. At the identical spot to where she had been the effect was quite astonishing. Though I strained every muscle, I could not prevent the hazel from forcing itself round in my hands. Standing there proudly and rubbing the sore skin on the palms of my hands, I knew that if all else failed and the ducks never laid, at least there was one other possible career open to me.

It was late by then and, since we were staying nearby, we asked whether we could come over again and have another look round the following morning.

Chapter Two

By July, 1964, we were the proud owners of Daw's Hall. Although we had no intention of putting on any lavish extensions or doing anything else that would change the character of the house, it was clear that some modernization was necessary. The surveyor's report had indicated that certain things like the plumbing were a trifle archaic but, worse still, that hosts of evil insects had apparently infested the woodwork. There were so many things to do, both inside and outside the house, that at first we were not sure to whom to turn. We need not have worried. All too soon we discovered tht there exists a whole army of people who, for varying financial considerations, are only too pleased to rush in and help. Most of them just appeared on the doorstep. There were electricians, drainage experts, pest control officers, installers of burglar alarms, landscape gardeners and purveyors of everything from parquet flooring to fire extinguishers. Interspersed among their visiting cards was a request for financial contributions from a charity devoted to the welfare of stray cats, an invitation from the rector to supply home-made jam for the Church fête and another from the Jehovah's Witnesses to allow them to save our souls.

Then d'Esterre met a very noisy female at a cocktail party, who said how on earth could we possibly manage without an architect and that she knew just the right person for us. 'Apparently he's just finished renovating 10 Downing Street,' d'Esterre announced importantly. Adding, when she sensed my lack of enthusiasm over getting involved in any further expense, 'Just think, it'll take so many worries off your shoulders and you'll be able to get on with your duck ponds.' When Ronnie arrived the following morning, I soon realized that the reputation architects have for being

Daw's Hall.

incorrigible and insidious seducers was far from being unfounded.
Part of the conversation that first day went something like this:

R. Well — first things first — let's have a look at the kitchen, by
far the most important room in any house.

I.G. (*Meekly*): What about my dressing room?

R. (*turning his back on me and casting conspiratorial glances at
my wife*): You know, it never pays to economize over
kitchens. You'd be surprised for instance how many people
make the mistake of not having enough cupboards.
Personally I feel, and I'm sure you'd agree with me, Mrs
Grahame, that twenty-eight cupboards is the bare minimum
for an efficient, labour-saving kitchen.

D'E. But of course, and (*slight pause*) do please call me d'Esterre.

R. How kind of you, d'Esterre, (*adding, as if we didn't know*)
I'm Ronnie. Now, we'll have to sort out the best place for a
built-in oven, hob units, twin sinks, deep freeze, washing-up
machine, concealed lighting...

I.G. (*helplessly*): But I can't afford all those things!

R. My dear fellow, I know it's difficult for you to understand,

18

but these things aren't luxuries, they're essentials. Just think of the saving to d'Esterre in time and labour.

I.G. I...

R. Look, old chap, I don't want to waste your valuable time. Wouldn't it be better to let d'Esterre and me sort out these little details on our own?

When I got back from scything down the nettles, they were sitting cosily together at the top of the stairs, sipping my best Moselle and discussing colour schemes for our bedroom.

'Oh, darling, Ronnie's been *such* a help,' she announced happily. 'He's just been telling me where we can buy the most fabulous French wall-paper for your dressing room.' As many a better man before me had doubtless done in the face of this irresistible Casanova, I gave up the unequal struggle.

One thing was obvious: since central heating had to be installed, drains, plumbing and electrical wiring all redone, damp rot and death-watch beetle removed, to say nothing of Ronnie's brainwaves, the house was going to be uninhabitable for months. We decided, therefore, to make the cottage our temporary base. The trouble with the cottage was that it had only one cold tap and no sanitation or electricity. While the builders were doing a rushed job to install these essentials, we rented a room in a local pub. It was a very good pub, far too good in fact, as we discovered every Saturday night. My advice to anyone contemplating taking up a similar abode, for however short a period of time, is to select an establishment with a nightly attendance not exceeding three; and, if this is not possible, *never* accept a room over the Public Bar and *always* carry a near lethal dose of sleeping pills. Anyway, our particular pub, despite these minor inconveniences, at least had the advantage of being only four miles from Daw's Hall, and from it we conducted daily excursions, d'Esterre for her assignations with architect and builder, I to supervise the bulldozer and dragline.

With the assistance of a kind man from the Water Board, a scheme had been drawn up for the construction of two further ponds of generous dimensions, linked to each other and to the ghost-ridden pond in the wood by land-drains. Uphill from there, where we had done our water divining, our plan was to excavate the soil and make two parallel channels of water. These, dammed at intervals, would provide a constant, spring-fed supply of clean

19

water that would pass in turn through the main pond, the island pond and the bottom pond. It looked marvellous on paper. The big question was would it work?

I had engaged the services of a local contractor and, shortly after we had taken possession of the house, he moved in with his machines. They started on the two channels and for every bucketful of soil that was removed, more lovely fresh water rushed in to take its place. It was very exciting and even Ronnie, who occasionally minced his way down through the mud to see how we were getting on, voiced his approval. 'It really is absolutely super, old chap. I say, what about my drawing up a plan for an oriental folly, perched on a tiny island on this pond? It would look divine and we could all row out to it in the evening and have a glass or two of dry martini surrounded by exotic mandarin ducks.'

Apart from pond construction, the other urgent task was to put up the fox-proof fence all round the perimeter. Once this was completed, and the heavy machinery had departed, I knew that we should be ready to accept delivery of our first livestock. I had already placed two orders, one with the Colonel and the other with the Wildfowl Trust, for about fifty pairs of ornamental ducks and geese, informing them both that I hoped to be ready to receive them some time in October.

I had eight weeks in which to get ready. To help with the fencing, I had taken on two students on holiday in Sudbury. None of us had had any previous experience — the erection of heavy gauge wire fencing was sadly not included in the curriculum at Cirencester — so it was very much a case of the blind leading the blind. John, Richard and I worked flat-out on that fence for a month. The weather was marvellous and during that whole period we had no rain at all. Wearing only shorts, we were soon the colour of Red Indians. The severe drought that year made the sinking of the angle-iron posts into the ground extremely hard. Each one — and there were over three hundred of them — had to be buried two foot into the ground. Since the tops were bent at a forty-five degree angle (to prevent any predator from climbing over the fence) they could not be knocked in with a sledge hammer. Instead, a hole had to be dug for each one with a rabbiting spade and, having inserted the post, we filled in the hole with concrete, which was mixed and barrowed by hand. When the four weeks had gone by and six hundred and fifty yards of nine foot high wire netting had been put up, and innumerable gallons of good Suffolk ale put down, there was not an inch of flab on any of us.

During that month, the four acres of cordon apples in the old orchard were grubbed up and the field ploughed and harrowed in preparation for a crop of Christmas trees, the channels feeding the main pond were dammed and the land-drains linking the three ponds were laid. The island pond and bottom pond had been successfully excavated and we anxiously awaited some rain for them to fill up. Most important of all, the cottage saw the first bathroom, lavatory and electric light bulb in its four hundred years of existence. D'Esterre and I took up residence. The work on the house, however, seemed to drag on interminably. Having never previously employed architects or builders, we were learning for the first time that they are a law unto themselves when it comes to estimating the cost and duration of a job.

Before they went back to school, John and Richard helped me with the final preparations for the birds. Three foot high fences were put up to surround each separate pen and every inch of wire netting, including the perimeter fence, was given a thick coating of tar. This not only helped to camouflage what must be one of the most hideous of man-made objects, but also, we hoped would extend its life. I had been given this tip by an experienced aviculturist, but had stupidly mislaid his address and telephone number. And so, while the procuring of a drum of tar had been a simple enough operation, none of us could fathom out how it should be applied. First, we tried spraying it on, but the jets kept getting clogged up, and ninety per cent of the liquid passed straight through the wire netting and landed on the nettles on the far side of the fence. A four-inch paint-brush, while treating the nettles somewhat more leniently, flicked most of the tar back onto us, so that we soon resembled a trio of Dalmation dogs. Ronnie finally came to our assistance and introduced us to a paint roller. I was so pleased that I immediately sanctioned five extra cupboards for the kitchen.

At last the great day dawned for the arrival of the first birds. D'Esterre and I set off early to the Colonel's in a mini van and a car to collect them. It was a strange and rather uncomfortable feeling going back to the place where it had all started. We stopped briefly on the bridge, just as I had done almost exactly a year before, and there was the same pair of Hottentot teal and the other birds which this time I had no problem in recognizing. On this occasion I found myself looking at everything far more critically. Holes in the fencing and odd birds that were of dubious origin or not completely healthy quickly caught my eye. Somehow the place had lost its fairy-tale quality, or was it just that I had come to realize, during the last couple of months, the appalling amount of sweat and hard labour that goes into the creation and maintenance of a successful waterfowl farm?

I had fully expected to find the Colonel denuding his peacocks but this time he was pinioning a batch of late hatched Bahama pintails. A quick snip with a pair of nail-scissors and there were eight little ducklings that would never be able to fly. A brief squeak announced the severing of each wing joint — only the one wing is cut to create loss of balance — but the next moment they had forgotten all about it and were busy guzzling duckweed.

'Yes?' he snapped, just as he had done the previous year.

'Good morning, Colonel. Sorry we're a little late. May I introduce my wife?' I was certainly not going to be put off by the barrack-room bark this time.

'I don't think I know who you... Oh, yes, I do. Of course, you're Brown, Yorkshire Light Infantry, wasn't it?'

'The name's Grahame and I was a Green Jacket,' I announced rather pompously.

'Dammit yes, of course,' replied the Colonel. 'You must know my old friend "Braces" Brinkman, what?'

Since the officer in question had, to the best of my knowledge, passed away in India about the same year as I had been born, I saw little point in prolonging these military reminiscences and asked instead whether our birds were boxed up.

'They're all ready, old boy, just over there,' and he pointed to three neat ranks of cardboard boxes, each of which had previously been occupied by a dozen bottles of a well-known brand of gin. A pintail drake, I noticed, was trying to get out of one box. 'Nothing left to do but write your cheque, old chap. Oh, and by the way, I'd be most grateful if you'd put your name and address on the back.'

'Gosh,' whispered d'Esterre as we were loading up the two vehicles, 'He seems awfully keen to put you in your place, doesn't he?'

I shrugged my shoulders and suggested that perhaps it was because we were now considered potential rivals in the trade,

A pintail drake was trying to get out of one of the gin boxes.

rather than just prospective customers.

'Oh well, he certainly had the last word, making you put your name and address on the back of the cheque.'

'That's just where you're wrong,' I laughed, 'I wrote "Brown, Yorkshire Light Infantry"!'

I led our little convoy home and although it was only about thirty miles the journey took close on three hours. Ghastly thoughts kept coming into my head. Were the air holes big enough? Would the birds slip a tendon every time we went round a corner? What if they were asphyxiated by gin fumes? Every couple of miles I got out to check. When we eventually drew up at Daw's Hall, I felt, and probably looked, as though I had just returned from leading an allied convoy through U-boat infested waters. D'Esterre just looked fed-up.

Gingerly we off-loaded each of the boxes and carried them down to the edge of the main pond. D'Esterre cut the string round each of them and I folded back the lids. The birds, thankful that their ordeal in the Colonel's gin boxes was over, scurried off in every

23

direction. Huge white snow geese tried hopelessly to camouflage themselves under the laurel bushes, wood ducks attempted frantically to clamber up the wire netting, small teal quickly disappeared in the undergrowth and not a single bird went onto the water. D'Esterre and I looked at one another in puzzled amazement.

'Perhaps they know the pond is haunted,' she said after a moment or two. 'Do you think the parson would agree to exorcize it?'

We both looked accusingly at the pond and I almost expected to see long blond tresses surfacing through the duckweed. A pair of red-crested pochard had come out of their hiding place and were standing close to the water's edge.

'Come on,' I said. 'Let's drive them in and I'm sure the others will follow.'

We edged our way quietly round behind and then advanced towards them. The two ducks eyed us carefully and then, realizing that they had no option, tried to get into the water. The duckweed, however, was so thick that they just walked rather self-consciously out into the middle. Then, recognizing the gastronomic possibilities, they lowered their bills into it and proceeded to eat.

Two pairs of snow geese took it at a run disrupting the blue-winged teal.

After a few moments there were two little plops as the weed gave way beneath them and, finally in the water, they guzzled away furiously at the vast sea of green that surrounded them. Gradually we succeeded in rounding up the rest of the collection and driving them into the pond. The smaller ducks took far longer to eat their way through into the water, but with the larger birds it was quite different. The two pairs of snow geese, flushed from their hiding place, took it at a run, honking with obvious alarm. As they left dry land, the weed parted momentarily beneath them before they disappeared entirely from view. A little party of blue-winged teal that had been feeding quietly nearby vanished simultaneously in the eruption. Seconds later they all reappeared a few feet away with greenery hanging from their plumage. Eventually they were all located and, with the pond reverberating to the happy dabbling of waterfowl, d'Esterre and I repaired to the cottage for our bread and cheese.

That afternoon, the second consignment from the Wildfowl Trust arrived, this time by passenger train to our local railway station. Within forty-eight hours the combined activities of almost a hundred voracious beaks succeeded in stripping the pond of its last vestige of duckweed.

Although the cottage was perfectly comfortable, we were both now anxious to get into the house as soon as possible. Our first child was expected early in the new year, and I could not employ a full time assistant until we had accommodation to offer him.

Ronnie, as soon as he realized that d'Esterre's weight increase was not caused by over-eating, insisted on a third bathroom and an enormous airing cupboard for dealing with nappies, while I continued unsuccessfully to look for ways in which we could economize. One obvious method was to do some of the decorating ourselves.

One afternoon, with our two dogs for company, I made a start on the spare bedroom. All went well until a mouse jumped out of the cupboard and in the ensuing commotion the dogs knocked over my can of paint. The next day, after the birds had been fed and the builders had knocked off, I went up to the house on my own. I had been happily splashing white emulsion paint on the ceiling for about half an hour when I became aware of a dog padding up and down the ground floor passage. I stopped and listened and after about thirty seconds it stopped. There was nothing eerie about the noise; it was still broad daylight, yet it was inexplicable: I had left our labrador and dachshund with d'Esterre at the cottage, and I had very deliberately shut the back door after I had come into the house. It momentarily crossed my mind that the front door might have been left open by the builders. Just as I was trying to think of some obvious explanation, the noise started again. 'Eider, Dezzie....,' I called. Had one or both of the dogs got into the house, perhaps through a window? No response, and I must confess that at that stage I experienced a slightly spine-chilling sensation. Putting down my paintbrush, I started cautiously down the back stairs to investigate, but had only got down a couple of steps when the noise stopped. I lit a cigarette and sat down on the staircase to await developments, but absolutely nothing happened, so I then walked round the house checking all the doors and windows. Every one was closed. From there I went down through the vegetable garden to the cottage. Eider and Dezzie were fast asleep in their baskets and d'Esterre confirmed that they had been there since I had left.

A week or two later we went to a cocktail party in the village and I was telling our neighbouring farmer about what had happened.

'I'm not at all surprised,' he said. 'Didn't you know that your house was haunted by a dog?'

'I certainly did not,' I replied truthfully: 'We've been told about the woman who was drowned in the pond, but this is the first I've heard about a ghost dog. I didn't even know such things existed!'

'Why don't you write to your predecessors?' he suggested. 'They knew all about it and I believe somebody who was staying there once saw it. I'm pretty sure it was a whippet.'

A few days later we received the following reply to our letter:—

'When we first went to Daw's we had an Aberdeen terrier and she slept on the top back passage at the head of the stairs. One night she howled violently and would not go back to her bed to sleep, nor would she go there again for several days. Later — she had to be destroyed as she killed chickens — we had a springer and she had her bed in the same place. On one occasion she howled in the night and wouldn't sleep there again. Then our second springer did the same.

'I had an old "adopted" aunt, very matter of fact, and one day when she came downstairs she said to me "I didn't know you had another dog, Ruby."

"Another dog, Aunt Jess?"

26

"Yes, the whippet."

"What whippet?"

"The whippet I saw just now sleeping at the top of the stairs." I laughed and said she must have been dreaming...'

Each evening, when I went up to the house to carry on with the decorating, sometimes on my own and sometimes with d'Esterre, I secretly hoped that I would hear the dog again. Nothing, however, happened. Then, one afternoon, the newspaper delivery man from the neighbouring village, who was doing odd carpentry jobs for me, saw me drive up to the house from a local meeting that I had had to attend. As I stepped out of the car, he looked more and more startled, as though he could not believe his eyes.

'What's up, Jack?' I asked. 'You look as if you've seen a ghost.'

'Oi down roightly know about seein' a ghost, but oi reckons as oi've bloody 'eard 'un. Blasted noisy bugger he were tew.'

He then explained that he had been looking for me to discuss some point of detail about the chicken shed and had thought I might be in the house. Hearing a lot of noise coming from what was to be the library he had walked along the passage and knocked on the door. The noise coming from inside had apparently been almost deafening, as though a lot of heavy furniture was being shifted around. He had knocked again, as loud as he could and then, since there was no reply, he had walked out of the house and looked in through the window. Having seen there was nobody in the room, he had reckoned that I must have slipped out of the other door while he was walking round.

D'Esterre, to whom I related this latest incident, was thoroughly sceptical. Although I tried to explain to her that, until that afternoon when I had heard the dog, I had always taken any ghost story with a large pinch of salt, nothing would convince her that there was not some logical explanation for both these incidents. So, I was really quite glad when the next manifestation happened to her. She was putting up curtains in the house one morning when she became aware of a nasty burning smell. It was, she told me, as though the house was on fire. She immediately rushed round every room but found that all was well. When she mentioned this to our neighbour's wife, she learned that the same thing had happened on many occasions, always at the same time of year, to our predecessors. It was, apparently, the anniversary of

27

when the house had burned down.

The only other inexplicable thing that happened during our early days at Daw's Hall was trivial but tiresome. Again, it was in the library, which was in the old part of the house. As everyone knows, the larger a chimney, the more rubbish it collects. This particular chimney served two Tudor fireplaces and when old jackdaw nests and other *débris* started to fall into the grate, we booked the services of the local chimney sweep. Since he was unable to come for a week or so, we put a larger fender across the fireplace to keep the new carpet clean.

It was my first job in the morning, before feeding the birds, to walk up from the cottage to the house to check that all was well. One morning, when I walked into the library, I saw that a lot of rubbish had come down the chimney in the night and a large lump of soot had finished up in one of the armchairs close to the fireplace. The fire guard was still in position. Somewhat mystified, I chucked the soot into the grate and pushed both armchairs over towards the window. The next morning there was an even larger lump in each of them.

If Daw's Hall was haunted, it certainly did not affect us in any material way, nor did we ever have any regrets about buying the place. Ronnie and the builders were doing all sorts of wonderful things to the house, the birds had settled down and become delightfully tame and our paranormal experiences were lively topics at every dinner party that we went to. The feeding every day of the birds occupied comparatively little time, but there was an immense amount of other work to be done. The areas around the island pond and bottom pond had to be sown with grass seed, the banks levelled and protected with concrete; there were dividing fences to be erected, long grass to be scythed, trees and shrubs to be planted and preparations to be made for the first breeding season.

Our visits to the Wildfowl Trust and other collections, together with avid reading of a great many books and articles in magazines, had given me a rough idea of the basic requirements. With few exceptions, all species of waterfowl nest during the English spring and early summer. Geese are generally excellent parents, guarding their eggs and goslings with the utmost bravery, but most ducks are notoriously bad mothers. Clutches, while varying considerably between breeds, average around eight to ten eggs and it is only too common to see a large happy family of ducklings rushing around

28

like bumblebees on the water being daily reduced in numbers. There are many different causes for their high mortality — bad weather, foxes, moorhens, pike and so on — and nature sees to it that in such cases the parents attempt a second, third or even fourth clutch. But even so, only the ubiquitous mallard and black duck seem to increase to any marked extent. Though ducks properly kept in captivity and protected against vermin avoid many of their natural enemies in the wild, they are faced with a further problem in rearing their young successfully, and this is the lack of natural food. Unless the area of their confinement is excessively generous and contains plenty of fresh-water insects and aquatic plants, starvation is a common cause of death, since the babies are not likely to take readily to the food given to their parents. Furthermore, in a mixed collection, other adult birds will often set upon ducklings and drown them. For these reasons the accepted practice among all serious waterfowl breeders is to carry out artificial hatching and rearing of these birds.

I am always amazed at the widespread ignorance among many country people, young and old alike, over some of the simpler facts of nature. One popular fallacy is that butterflies only live for a day: another, that the incubation of an egg starts from the moment that it is laid. If the latter were true, I for one would certainly give up eating eggs for breakfast. The eggs are normally laid at one or two day intervals and the mother duck will often spend the greater part of the day on the nest. The embryo in each egg, which is at first too small to be seen with the naked eye, remains in a dormant state until the clutch is complete and the parent bird commences incubation. Her body during this period generates a temperature reading of somewhere between 98 and 103 degrees fahrenheit and gradually the embryos develop until, after three or four weeks, depending on the species, out pop the ducklings.

Techniques for artificial simulation of this process are dependent either on an incubator or a broody hen. For the very simple reason that with most biological functions nature is best, many breeders of ornamental waterfowl prefer to have their hatching done by broodies. This was the method that I decided to adopt, anyway for a start. Consequently, while d'Esterre was occupied with putting the finishing touches to cradles and matinée jackets, Jack and I were equally busy converting an old apple-shed into a chicken-house, providing an appropriate area

29

for the nest boxes and procuring a suitable strain of poultry.

My Cirencester notes contained the most elaborate designs for the construction of huge and horrible edifices wherein hybrid chickens (with their inevitable abbreviated nomenclature) would be expected to churn out millions of tasteless eggs every year, or to finish up as 'farm-fresh' and 'oven-ready' in the supermarkets. Nowhere could I find a single reference to buildings for housing a good old-fashioned flock of Light Sussex, Rhode Island Reds or Silkies, that would not only scrabble around in the hen run but, hopefully, be capable of hatching their own and others' eggs.

I invited the gamekeeper from my old home, the man from whom almost everything that I knew about the countryside had been learned, to come over and look round the farm. Together we planned the design of the hatching and rearing equipment, and devised methods for dealing with stoats, magpies and other vermin. The blue-prints were then passed on to Jack who, apart from the one interruption of the ghost in the library, busied himself for three afternoons a week with the detailed carpentry required. By Christmas the chicken house, nest boxes and rearing units were completed and I was the proud possessor of six dozen healthy, happy chickens and a quartet of wildly oversexed cockerels, none of which appeared to belong to any known breed. My proudest moment each afternoon was when I carried down to the cottage the daily quota of delicious fresh eggs that my mongrel flock provided.

It might be imagined that apart from the normal bills, an occasional supernatural manifestation and periodic income tax demands, there was little to disturb the peace of this busy but idyllic existence. My sheltered career as an army officer and more recently as an antediluvian student had so far succeeded in keeping me in blissful isolation from that predatory band of officials, who are apparently exempt from sticking postage stamps onto their envelopes and merely substitute the sinister initials OHMS. How anyone in the Ministry of Agriculture, Fisheries and Food heard that I ran a commercial business that came under their aegis I shall never know. Perhaps one of our neighbours had complained at the dawn chorus in which my randy cockerels vociferously indulged. Or maybe our smart new sign announcing the presence of Daw's Hall Wildfowl Farm had caught the eye of some snooping official. Anyway, within a fortnight of the arrival of my little flock of poultry, I received a document inviting me to list in detail every farm animal that we kept. Most of it applied only to cattle, sheep and pigs, but there were sections dealing with poultry and other livestock that had to be completed. Under 'breed of poultry' I entered, perfectly honestly, 'don't know', while for the waterfowl I decided to blind them with science, listing the Latin names of all our birds. Then, a small section at the bottom of the form caught my attention. Did I wish to claim any grants — land drainage, grubbing up of orchards, etc? I had recently, at enormous expense, got a contractor to bulldoze out and burn four acres of apple trees that had produced no fruit for several years. Now it appeared that OHMS was actually offering to reimburse me. Clearly I had been maligning these generous and helpful people. With the assistance of an old razor blade I scratched out 'don't know' against my poultry and substituted 'hybrid varieties'. To the section dealing with agricultural and horticultural grants, I wrote 'yes, please.'

A week or so later a small deputation from the Ministry came and called on us. An elderly spinster introduced herself as being responsible for poultry management and diseases in the district, while her companion, an earnest young man with an enormous briefcase, announced that he had come to discuss any financial grants to which we might be entitled. I took them on a conducted tour of the premises. Much to my surprise, the poultry lady was thrilled to see my free-range chickens and, apart from a very helpful and justified criticism of the ventilation in their building, congratulated me on their management. She also gave me the name and address of a reliable breeder of Silkie bantams, which she considered to be the best potential broodies of all. Leaving her with d'Esterre, Ronnie and a decanter of sherry, I then set off with the male member of the party. He explained that I was certainly eligible for a grant, but that the actual amount of money forthcoming depended on the average circumference of the trees that we had removed. He also pointed out that I should have made my application while the apple trees were still standing. Some of the larger trees had in fact not been consumed by the bonfire that the contractor had made and it was to these that he applied a tape measure from his briefcase.

'Pretty borderline,' he announced after fumbling among the charred remains for a little while. 'A pity, really. We only need another inch on average all round and you'll qualify for an even

31

higher grant.'

Frantically, I scrabbled among the ashes for some larger pieces but soon decided that, as his pinstripe suit was deteriorating every minute that we prolonged the search, it was time to be thankful for small mercies and to repair to the cottage for alcoholic refreshment. The grant that arrived was particularly exciting as it was the first item that I could record in the receipts side of my farm accounts. A month or so later a crop of twenty thousand Norway spruce trees were planted in the field, and it was a great thrill to realize that I had actually embarked on my first forestry enterprise.

I have always had a love of trees and it had been my ambition one day to plant my own arboretum. Daw's Hall was blessed with some magnificent, mature specimens and, since the land not devoted to the birds was of too small an acreage to consider any agricultural crop, it seemed only natural to plant any trees that had economic possibilities. Apart from the Norway spruces that were destined for the Christmas tree market, we put one field down to poplars and another to Scots pine, oak and beech. I calculated that the pine trees might be a useful cash crop for my grandchildren, while the hardwood trees were my small contribution to posterity in the twenty-second century.

That winter, a neighbouring smallholder retired and his place came on the market. The house was sold separately, but we were lucky enough to be able to buy another fifteen acres, thereby doubling the size of our holding and giving us an extremely attractive area of water-meadows bordering the Stour. It was an enchanting and unspoint area with good coarse fishing in the river and wonderful beds of nettles for butterflies on the banks. A pair of kingfishers had nested in the river bank that summer. This latest acquisition was put down to cricket bat willows.

Salix caerulea is the best willow for bats and has long been planted for this purpose in eastern England. The original tree is said to have been found in Norfolk in about 1700. Although rooted trees are sometimes planted, the usual practice is to push an unrooted set about two feet into the ground where, if the soil is sufficiently damp, it will soon strike and form its own roots. Thereafter, the only work entailed is keeping the stem clean by brushing off any green shoots that appear up to a height of at least seven foot. After about fifteen years the tree is felled and sold to a bat willow merchant who cuts it into rolls and later into clefts from which the bat itself is shaped. The majority of cricket bats used all over the world originate from trees grown in East Anglia.

During that first winter d'Esterre, who was growing visibly larger every day, was understandably more concerned with impending maternity benefits than horticultural grants. A tiny nursery had been prepared at the cottage, decorated in mixed pink and blue to allow for either eventuality, and the services of a monthly nurse engaged. By mid-January preparations were finalized for the hatching season on both fronts.

The first birth recorded at Daw's Hall Wildfowl Farm occurred on the twenty-sixth of January 1965. Angus Robert Grahame came into the world, screaming lustily, and the cottage was soon an organised chaos of bottles and nappies.

Chapter Three

Shortly after Angus was born the ducks decided it was time for them to think about breeding. As the weather started to get a little warmer they began to indulge in feverish exhibitions of affection towards their mates and equally furious displays of agression to any potential rivals. 'Love thy neighbour,' was clearly not a maxim observed at this time of year among waterfowl.

Jack and I had made a number of nest boxes, including some special ones for the Carolinas and mandarins which almost invariably make nests high up in cavities of trees in the wild. Being pinioned, our birds were provided with rustic step-ladders to enable them to climb up to these boxes, which were placed against various trees surrounding the main pond.

Most birds are extremely secretive over their nesting sites, so it was with some surprise that I watched the highly comical antics of these two species of duck. Although there were fifteen boxes and only twelve pairs of wood ducks, they behaved like small children squabbling over the same toy. The popular choice was a box against the big cedar tree. Early each morning the couples would gather beneath it and the pantomime started with a general chorus of chattering and display in which they all joined. Ethnologists call this 'epigamic motor display patterns and vocalizations', but I personally prefer the more mundane whistle-sneezing for the Carolina, and burping in the case of the mandarin. Whenever the gentlemen stopped to draw breath from this monotonous form of conversation, the ladies would, usually by indicating a possible rival for their affections, incite them to begin the burps and whistle-sneezes afresh. After a while, one of the wives would venture coyly up the ladder and into the box, closely followed by

Carolina's and mandarins play at I'm the King of the Castle.

her husband who would take up poisition on top of the lid. Act II was entitled 'I'm the King of the Castle,' or 'How to get rid of squatters'. The opposing males, egged on by their womenfolk, would charge up the ladder and endeavour to evict the incumbents. The fellow on top of the box, encouraged by his mate inside, would rush down to repel boarders and there on the ladder the battle would take place. The finale came when one or both of the contestants toppled off and fell to the ground. Sometimes a couple, anxious to solve the housing problem on their own, would sidle off from the general *mêlée* and occupy a different nest box. Not for long, however, were they left in peace. The whole throng would move across to the new site and there the pantomime started all over again.

The courtship displays of the other ducks were equally fascinating to watch, but these were normally confined to the water and in no way advertised the presence of any nest. We had pairs of all three species of wigeon and our favourites were the Chiloë wigeon with beautiful metallic-green markings on their heads and chestnut coloured flanks. They were among the most garrulous of all our birds, chattering and whistling lovingly to each other all day long. When particularly excited, the male and female, which are almost identical in plumage, would take part in frantic nodding sessions to each other, culminating in a long drawn-out whistle call by the male that sounds remarkably like their name. The resemblance is quite fortuitous, for their name is, in fact, derived from the island of Chiloë off Southern Chile where they are still extremely common. Another favourite was the Bahama pintail, of which we had a little flock of ten, including two albinistic birds, which are commonly known as silver Bahamas. Like the Northern pintails, their cousins from Europe and Asia, the Bahamas are remarkably silent birds, though the drakes do make rather muted and genteel burps during the main display, which is characterized by the males cocking their tails up over their backs. The falcated drake, with his incredibly beautiful purple and green headpiece and flowing, silvery extensions to his wings, was another of our ducks with a very similar display pattern.

Our diving ducks on the whole were more subdued in their courting, although one particular red-crested pochard drake, who we christened Barbarossa on account of his fiery red hair and filthy temper, was continually trying to muscle in on two perfectly happily married tufted ducks. Whenever they were quietly swimming around together he would rush in between them and try and drown poor Mr Tufty. The latter, however, being a far more proficient underwater swimmer, never had any difficulty in giving his pursuer the slip. He would merely dive down under the water where he remained for an incredibly long time while Barbarossa wheezed and sneezed angrily on the surface while trying to guess at which point Mr Tufty would next emerge.

The males of some species are very noisy indeed, particularly the various forms of shelduck. But, generally, it is the females who are more vociferous than the males and it is only the females that quack. Tommy Johnstone at Slimbridge had told me that this is one of the easiest ways of sexing young birds before they come into their adult plumage. If you pick up a duck and shake it around long enough, it will usually say, in ducky language and with suitable ducky expletives, 'For God's sake, put me down.' The males do this by a variety of hoarse mutterings, hisses and wheezes, while the females, if they say anything at all, quack. One does, of

Barbarossa, a red-crested pochard drake, tried to upset the marriage of two tufted ducks.

course, meet birds tht are too scared or too stubborn to say anything and the only reliable way of determining their gender is to peer in oriental fashion up their anal orifices.

Apart from Barbarossa, who was really more of a fool than a blackguard, there was one duck that did seriously threaten to disrupt the general harmony on the main pond and that was Cocky, a male Cape teal. He was only half the size of many of the other birds and he had a deceivingly soft grey plumage and pink *retroussé* bill. His eyes, however, were the clue to his character. They literally flashed with fire. No adversary was too large for Cocky to tackle and what surprised me was the submissive way they reacted to him. He seemed to have an uncontrollable desire to drown every other bird in sight, males and females alike. Then I noticed that Clara Bow, a pert and flirtaceous Chilean teal whom he was frequently on top of in the water, was not just being drowned out of hand but actually raped. Cocky, to cap all his other atrocities, had now shown himself in his true colours. He was a lascivious and brutal sex maniac. Since I had no wish to have little Cockies popping out of every egg that was laid and rampaging all over the farm, he clearly had to be removed. More than once I had considered using my shotgun on him, but d'Esterre very sensibly suggested that he and Mrs Cocky be caught up and penned in an empty enclosure above the main pond. The finishing touches were put to this pen and all that remained was to catch the birds. We had a trout landing net which seemed suitable and, since the birds were all very tame, I saw little difficulty in popping it over Cocky and his wife at feed time.

That afternoon I laid my plans carefully. The net was placed against a bay bush close to the pond and I waited until it was almost dark before feeding so that the birds would be particularly keen to come onto the land and have their tea. As I sauntered casually down with the bucket of corn, my eye was on one bird and one bird only. While most of the other ducks were soon clustered around me and feeding hungrily, Cocky, Clara Bow and one or two others remained on the water. I gave my usual whistle and rattled the bucket. Clara Bow and Mrs Cocky soon rushed up to join us. In a flash I had dropped the bucket, grabbed the net and put it over the lecher's lawful wife. It was a terrible mistake. All the other birds fled into the water with cries of alarm and were so put out by my duplicity that for several days they would only come out to feed after I had left. During this period, with Mrs Cocky safely away from home, Cocky's carnal lust knew no bounds and many of my young ladies didn't stand a chance.

After a week, the birds appeared to have settled down and I decided it was time to have another go. I missed out the morning feed so that by late afternoon the birds were ravenously hungry, and many of them were waiting for me by the gate, a good fifty yards from the pond, when I came in to feed them. Needless to say, Cocky was not among them. By feeding the chickens first and pottering around longer than usual in the hen-house, I prolonged their wait still further. Then, as darkness was beginning to fall, I walked down to the main pond. The pigeons were coming in to roost in the oak trees and a green woodpecker flew off with a loud laughing call from high up in the big cedar. Cocky, I noticed to my disgust, was brazenly having an affair with two Carolina ladies simultaneously, while their husbands hovered, burping anxiously, out of harm's reach. 'Come on, Cocky,' I called. 'Good little Cocky, time for tea.' And then, muffling my voice so that he would not hear, 'Let's have you, you horrible little sex maniac.' Much to my surprise and doubtless to that of the two Carolina drakes, he came instantly to my call. Quickly I checked on the position of the net and inched my way fractionally closer to it. I started to scatter the corn, keeping it well up on the bank and further from the water than usual. Cocky, rasping and hissing from his exertions, started to feed, though it was noticeable how everyone gave him an extremely wide berth. I was easing my way gradually between him and the pond when, quite suddenly, he looked up and his fiery little eyes met mine. He knew it was a trap and bolted towards the water straight between my legs. Just as he was passing through, I whipped round and threw myself bodily at him. The next thing I knew was that I was sitting up to my midriff in the pond holding Cocky firmly round his throat. Flushed with success, I reunited him with Mrs Cocky in their new pen, and marched triumphantly down to the cottage leaving a trail of slimy water behind me. D'Esterre, who was leaning out of Angus's nursery window, was unimpressed when I gave her the glad tidings and told me in no uncertain terms to remove my filthy clothes before coming indoors. I did as I was told and discarded everything on the back doorstep. Shivering with cold, I stepped inside and came face to face with the monthly nurse.

That year I knew that only one variety of our geese could possibly breed. These were a three year old pair of cereopsis. The others — barnacle, snow, lesser whitefront, bar-headed, Ross's and emperor — were still juveniles from whom we could expect no eggs for at least another couple of years. Water was now beginning to flow through the island pond and the grass that we had sown was growing well, so all these geese were moved down there.

Cereopsis, or Cape Barren geese, were once plentiful in the southern part of Australia but during this last century have been much persecuted by man. Not only is their flesh delicious to eat, but they also consume a great deal of grass and leave an odour which is apparently distasteful to sheep. They are now considered to be threatened with extinction and, as such, receive full protection. Like all endangered species, they deserve every possible encouragement to breed in captivity. When kept in the northern hemisphere they have the tiresome habit of laying in the middle of the winter. Surprisingly, they do exactly the same in Australia, breeding there between June and August.

The pugnacity of the ganders is well known and, although Henrietta was a quiet and docile creature, who grunted and snorted like a large white sow, her husband, Henry, was exactly the opposite. On arrival they had been given a separate pen with plenty of grass surrounded by the normal three foot high partition fencing. Henry, like Cocky, clearly disliked me intensely and on the few occasions that I went in to his pen he charged me like a bull, trumpeting loudly, and each time forced an ignominious retreat. During February, I saw them mating. This was very encouraging but it also meant that Henry's temper worsened still further. He must have regarded me as a potential rival, for every time I came near his pen he would race along the side of his enclosure and try to hit me with his wings and bite me with his parrot-shaped green bill through the wire. On the twentieth of February, Henrietta laid her first egg under a holly tree and Henry celebrated the occasion by leaping like a hurdler over his fence, knocking the bucket flying out of my hand and biting me severely in the leg. That morning I shut him up in the toolshed while I put an eighteen inch extension all round the top of their paddock. To my horror he very nearly cleared that the same afternoon.

During the first week of March there was a heavy fall of snow and the temperature dropped to several degrees below freezing. The

*With the temperature several degrees below freezing, our cereopsis
goose sat huddled on her eggs beneath the holly tree.*

ponds froze over so hard that I had to smash the ice twice a day with a pickaxe. The mandarins and Carolinas stopped jousting over the nest boxes and sat with the other birds on the ice trying vainly to thaw out their feet with their breast feathers. All this time poor Henrietta sat huddled on her four eggs beneath the holly tree. Their little pond of course was frozen too and each morning and afternoon I had to run the gauntlet when I went in to clear an area for them to drink.

Henrietta's routine was to come off the nest once a day, during the morning feed. After a noisy ritual of grunting and neck stretching with Henry, she would quickly eat, drink, preen her feathers and return to the nest. One morning she seemed very loath to go back onto her eggs and I could sense that all was not well. After about half an hour I went into the pen. Henry leapt straight at the most sensitive part of my anatomy but fortunately I succeeded in catching him in mid-flight before any damage was done. Holding him firmly by the wings with one hand and using a long stick in the other, I lifted Henrietta's down with the aid of the stick and saw that the four eggs had taken on a repulsive, mottled green hue and that feathers were sticking to some of them as though they were oozing. Bending down and holding the struggling Henry at arm's length, I picked each one up and sniffed it cautiously. The first three were addled. I was just holding the fourth close to my nose when Henry, who was no light-weight, struggled violently and somehow managed to smash this egg. It exploded like a bomb and splattered us both. From the sickening smell it was perfectly clear that no little Henry or Henrietta would have emerged from that egg either. It is on occasions such as these that one needs a third, or even fourth, arm. Dropping both stick and bird, one hand shot involuntarily up to grasp my nostrils, and with the other I endeavoured to brush my coat, while Henry, freed from my grasp, stood there thumping me lustily with his wings.

I hoped that after a little while the birds would select a different site and that Henrietta would lay a second clutch. The thaw came, the ice melted and the daffodils in the wood were a carpet of gold, but the cereopsis geese discarded their feathers and went into their moult.

We wondered who would nest next. Although there were still occasional squabbles among the mandarins and Carolinas on the step-ladders, most pairs appeared to have decided where they were

42

going to lay. It was the Carolinas on which I pinned most of my hopes, as I knew that mandarin ducks in their first year seldom lay fertile eggs. Other ducks too could be seen walking rather self-consciously along the hedgerows and peering into old beer barrels and hollow logs that I had put down to tempt them. Much to my fury, Clara Bow had settled for a divorce from her own husband and spent her whole time soliciting Cocky through the wire netting that now imprisoned him.

On the last day of March, while I was feeding the birds before breakfast, I noticed that Barbarossa was behaving in a very agitated fashion. He was standing on his own on the far side of the pond, making odd little noises and looking continually towards a big laurel bush that hung over the water's edge. Mrs Barbarossa was missing. If it had not been for him I am sure I would never have found that nest. She was immaculately camouflaged against the pile of dead leaves on which she was sitting. When she saw that I had seen her, she jumped off the nest and into the water and there were three lovely pale green eggs.

The next day I found the first Carolina nest and Mrs Barbarossa laid her fourth egg. I collected all five eggs and, carrying them as though they were priceless pieces of Dresden china, took them to the cellar up at the house. There I laid them very carefully, pointed end down, in a tray of sand that I had prepared for this purpose. On each egg I wrote the breed of bird and date laid. Then I went to the chicken house and collected five bantam eggs of roughly the same dimensions, put a 'D' for dummy on each and placed these in the two duck nests. Both birds immediately abandoned their nests, Mrs Barbarossa, or it could have been Barbarossa himself, emphasizing the point by hoofing their four dummy eggs into the pond. After this sad error of judgement, I decided to leave every nest undisturbed until the clutch was complete, hoping that no vermin would steal the eggs before I got to them. This, too, did not work out quite as planned. Although I thought that the wood ducks had resolved their housing problems, the nest box against the cedar tree was clearly receiving more than its fair share of attention. One Monday morning the first egg was laid there, the following day there were four and by the end of the week there were no less than twenty-three, the top layer flush with the hole half way up the box. These I took down to the cellar and all the wood ducks then turned their attention to a beer barrel on the opposite side of the main

43

pond. On more than one occasion, I was tempted to telephone the Colonel and ask his advice, but pride or pig-headedness always prevailed.

By mid-April, Angus had been christened in the little Norman church in the village, Ronnie had installed his final cupboard in the house and most of the summer migrants had arrived. Chiffchaffs, willow warblers, spotted flycatchers and blackcaps were building their nests in the wooded area round the main pond and in the still of the evenings a nightingale sang melodiously from a hazel thicket at the bottom of the lane. Swallows and house martins hawked for insects over the ponds and began to carry mud to the house for their nests. I noticed that the lawn badly needed mowing, that young shoots had to be rubbed off the bat willows, that the flower beds up at the house were a jungle of weeds and that my tiny Christmas trees were rapidly being drowned in a sea of couch grass. While d'Esterre spent every spare moment of the day in the garden, parking Angus in his pram under the shade of the tulip tree, I disappeared with a hoe into the Christmas tree field whenever time allowed. The trees were too small to use a rotovator between the rows and I had no wish to spray with chemicals, so there was no alternative but to hoe round all twenty thousand of them by hand. I must admit there were times when I doubted the wisdom of my aversion to pesticides, but when I saw brimstone and orange-tip butterflies hovering over the early spring flowers and kestrels and barn owls catching small rodents in the pine plantation, it was, somehow, all worthwhile. Often it was ten o'clock at night before I got back to the cottage with an aching back and blistered hands.

The population in the hen-house had recently been augmented by a dozen white Silkie bantams which I had got from the address recommended by the lady from the Ministry. Not only did they and the rest of my mongrel flock lay extremely well, but I now also had a number of birds that had gone broody. Shortly after the first duck egg had been laid I had transferred some of these onto china eggs in the brooder house. Early every afternoon they were lifted off their nests and given a quarter of an hour to eat, drink, dust themselves and defecate. They appeared to take to their false eggs and the routine very happily, unlike Mr and Mrs Barbarossa, and so, after a few days when they were obviously sitting tightly, I gave a couple of them ten bantam eggs apiece. The remaining four, after strict

44

injunctions to behave themselves properly, were given settings of red-crested pochard and Carolina eggs.

Other ducks were now beginning to nest — pintail, blue-winged teal, cinnamon teal and several pairs of wigeon. As the grass grew longer and the undergrowth thicker, it became increasingly difficult to find the nests. I actually trod on one teal that was sitting in a dense clump of cow-parsley but, miraculously, neither she nor her eggs were damaged.

The four cockerels had clearly not been wasting their time. After three weeks every single bantam egg hatched. The babies were black, white, brown and every possible combination of these colours. I left them for a day to harden off in the nest boxes and then, with the clucking mothers tucked under one arm and the twenty babies nestling together in the feedbucket suspended over my other arm, I took them outside to the brooders that Jack and I had made. Within minutes each family was happily feeding and drinking. I just hoped that my ducklings, if they hatched, would be as easy to manage.

Cecil, my old keeper friend, had told me that waterfowl eggs need a higher degree of humidity, particularly during the last few days before hatching, to help the ducklings to break through the tough membrane that lines the shell. As a child I had often helped him to sprinkle a little warm water over his pheasant and mallard eggs, especially when the weather was very hot and dry. I remembered, too, how we used sometimes to immerse a whole clutch of eggs in a bucket of warm water a day or so before they were due to chip. As I had recently discovered, duck and goose eggs emit a pernicious smell if they are addled and, as the egg shells are porous, this can literally asphyxiate the live inmates of other eggs in the clutch before they can emerge.

The pochard eggs were due off first and, when the time came for me to give the four eggs their pre-natal swim, it was fascinating to watch each one bobbing up and down on the surface. I knew then that they were all alive. The next day they were chipped, and while the bantam was having her lunch break I held each one in turn to my ear. I could hear the ducklings peeping away as they nibbled their tiny beaks at the shells. Cecil had told me years before that most birds (and reptiles too) have a little egg tooth to help them bite their way through to freedom and that this drops off or is absorbed shortly after they emerge.

The next day, when it was time to take the broodies off, I left the pochard eggs till last. When the other foster-mothers — and I then had more than a dozen birds sitting — were safely feeding, I tiptoed up to the boxes containing Mrs Barbarossa's eggs and put my ear to the air-holes on the door. Not a sound came out and I had a momentary vision of mass genocide within. Opening the box and putting my hand gently underneath her, I lifted the hen fractionally and there were four enquiring little pairs of eyes looking back at me. The ducklings were still rather damp so, hoping that the broody would not mind foregoing her lunch, I decided to leave the whole family in peace till the following day.

After all the birds were fed I had a break from hoeing Christmas trees and, instead, d'Esterre, Angus and I set off in the van with the two dogs, buckets and shrimping nets to a little pond in the next village. While Eider and Dezzie were frantically trying to catch a mole and Angus was gurgling happily at some private joke, d'Esterre and I paddled in the water in search of delicious morsels for the ducklings. It was not long before we had one bucket full of duckweed, and swimming around in the other was a marvellous selection of tadpoles, fresh-water shrimps, water-boatmen and other unidentified creatures. Back in the kitchen at the cottage, a series of small bowls and saucers was prepared and to our afternoon's catch were added chick crumbs, chopped lettuce and mashed hard-boiled egg. 'Looks *just* like all the things that we used to have with curry in Uganda,' d'Esterre remarked. Her analogy was appropriate, for we were having a few friends in to supper the following evening and planned to give them a good, hot curry. During the course of the party I was rash enough to recount the previous afternoon's experiences and to repeat d'Esterre's remark. One poor woman made an immediate retreat into the garden.

The excitement over the birth of the red-crested pochards was somewhat marred by the disappearance of their real mother. Mrs Barbarossa had not been seen for a couple of weeks and we presumed that she must have been killed by a rat or a stoat. I had spent hours searching for her in the undergrowth round the main pond but there was no trace of her. It was a complete mystery. Then, on the morning after our happy supper party, she suddenly reappeared on the pond with five babies in tow. Where she had nested we never discovered. I had not the heart to rob her of the babies at this stage and we just hoped that she would manage to

The first ducklings to hatch at Daw's Hall were red-crested pochards.

rear them successfully. My visions of a little flock of free-winged pochard flying round the farm were, however, abruptly shattered. That afternoon, when I came up to put their brothers and sisters out in a rearing pen, I saw to my dismay that there were only three on the water. It was not difficult to detect the cause of the trouble. Mr Tufty, doubtless determined to avenge the earlier affronts and abuses that he had sustained at the hands of Barbarossa, was waging a terrible retribution on the unfortunate ducklings. Barbarossa, to my disgust, was ignoring not only his wife and family but his old adversary too. He was currently trying to break up a marriage of two Bahama pintails. Fortunately, while I watched, Mrs Barbarossa and her surviving brood took refuge in a clump of day lilies growing on the bank and I was able to put the landing net over the lot of them. Mrs Barbarossa I returned to the pond in the hope that perhaps we might get another clutch from her, while the three squeaking infants joined their brothers and sisters under the bantam. The latter, after the initial shock of seeing her adopted family almost doubled at a stroke, was soon clucking protectively over all seven.

By midsummer we had over fifty ducklings. Mrs Barbarossa never laid again that year, but the Carolinas, pintails, shovellers and some of the wigeon and teal all had young being reared by the broodies, and Mrs Cocky and Mrs Tufty were both heavy with egg and were clearly going to lay. One afternoon, when I went into the broody shed for the daily exercising routine, I found a mystery duckling hatched and dry among a clutch of Carolina eggs that were not due to come off for another four or five days. There was no alternative but to try and join it up with the youngest batch of ducklings, which were some little blue-winged teal. I lifted the roof of the brooder and popped it in with them, but this particular bantam had no intention of being deceived that easily. She raised her hackles, churred angrily and made a vicious lunge at it with her beak. Quickly retrieving the defenceless baby, I carried it down to the cottage to discuss with d'Esterre what we should do next. Warmth, we both agreed, was the first requirement and the only alternatives that I could think of at that moment were d'Esterre's cleavage or the oven. It was clear from d'Esterre's reaction to my suggestions that it was going to be the oven. It was still warm from cooking lunch, so we adjusted the temperature reading to just under a hundred and popped our mystery bird inside with a little bowl of duckweed for nourishment.

'Well,' I said, 'that ought to keep it happy. All we've got to do now is to reduce the heat a little bit every day.'

'Every day?' She exclaimed in horror. 'If you think I'm going to have my oven occupied by an orphan duckling for the next fortnight you'd better think again. Apart from anything else, Angus's egg custard has got to be cooked in half an hour's time.'

'Well couldn't he have a tin of rice pudding heated up in a saucepan instead?' I suggested.

'No, he bloody well couldn't,' she replied with some vehemence.

'Poor little duckling,' I said. 'What on earth shall we do with it?'

It was d'Esterre who, in the end, came up with a thoroughly sensible solution. 'Why not pop it in a box in the airing cupboard?'

Archibald, for so he was christened, was kept beautifully warm in his new home and thrived on his diet of duckweed and egg. Whenever I came back to the cottage for a meal or at the end of the day, Archibald, who quickly recognized my voice, would greet me with high-pitched little squeaks of excitement and beg to be allowed out to join us. He was at his happiest when sitting on my shoulder under my shirt and if I leaned my head over to one side he would nibble my ear and chatter away affectionately. If I put him to the ground and walked away, he would rush after me as fast as his tiny legs could carry him, peeping plaintively and flapping his little wings to try and increase his speed. While our dachshund treated him with total contempt, Eider, the labrador, was devoted to him and loved it when he jumped up on top of her back as she lay in front of the stove. The other member of the household to whom he was very attached was Angus. After one occasion, however, when Angus, perhaps thinking Archibald was a particularly attractive squeaky toy, squeezed him rather hard and got a jet of green liquid in his eye, the relationship was discouraged.

There is only one time and one place where I demand total privacy and that is when I visit the lavatory immediately after breakfast. Even Archibald was forcibly restrained from joining me in this routine. Since, however, he always stood outside complaining loudly at his exclusion, I was never left in any doubt about the urgency of the operation.

The morning I decided it was time for him to have a swim, Archibald must have been mind-reading for he scrabbled down my shoulder and, much to our amusement, jumped headfirst into my bowl of cornflakes and milk. Much as he loved his morning swim (which to him must have been like bathing in Veuve Cliquot) it was a performance which, after a very few days, I began to discourage. Ducklings and all that goes with them grow at a remarkably fast rate. Archibald was provided with his own bowl of cornflakes.

That summer the farm produced a totally unexpected crop. One afternoon when I was tackling the weeds round what must have been about my fourteenth thousand Christmas tree, I heard talking and laughter from the other side of the hedge in the field which had been planted with young pines. Putting down my hoe and thankful for a respite, I walked across to investigate. There were about twenty women and children with plastic bags suspended from their necks busily picking handfuls of something which they were putting into the bags. I had noticed a week or two earlier that a mass of wild poppies were flowering in between the rows of trees and now, as I drew nearer to them, I could see that each bag was scarlet with poppy petals. They were most apologetic when I explained to them the field had recently changed hands. I then asked them what on earth they wanted poppies for, and one woman explained to me that a certain pharmaceutical manufacturing firm nearby paid them so much a pound for these petals which were apparently used in cough mixtures. Having one of my rare flashes of economic genius I told them that I would be back shortly, and I went to the cottage and telephoned the firm concerned. Yes, the man told me, they were indeed scouring the whole countryside in search of poppies and, since there was a terrible shortage that year, they were prepared to pay a very high price for them.

'How much?' I asked eagerly.

The figure that he gave me was exactly twice that mentioned by the woman in the field. I rushed back in a high state of glee to the pickers, telling them that they could pick as many petals as they liked, but that the bags must be handed over to me for delivery to the firm and that I would be responsible for paying them at the same rate. Thankful not to be evicted for trespassing and relieved that the tranportation was now taken off their shoulders, they redoubled their efforts and after a week I had sold no less than a quarter of a ton of this remarkable crop. I realized somewhat shamefacedly, while proudly making the second receipts entry in my farm accounts, that I had doubtless contributed in no small way to inflation in the cough mixture trade.

The nursery wing of the farm was growing at an alarming rate. Soon we were up to a hundred young waterfowl. All the little families had to be fed four times a day, and as we had already discovered with Archibald, ducklings were certainly not the cleanest of pets. Brooders, food bowls and so on had, therefore, to be frequently scrubbed. Ducklings are also remarkably stupid creatures, and there were several families of Carolinas in particular that appeared to be determined to commit suicide as quickly after birth as possible. Much to the consternation of their broody foster-mothers, they would either sit like scared mice in a corner getting rapidly chilled, or endeavour continually to jump up to the little wire-netting windows in their brooders, where they hung momentarily by one claw before toppling over onto their backs in the duckweed. I managed to save a few by force-feeding them with maggots suspended by d'Esterre's eyelash tweezers, but about a dozen literally starved themselves to death. Some of the most enchanting ducklings of all, and ones which never gave us any problems, were the offspring of Cocky and Mrs Cocky. D'Esterre's dressing table was, I regret to say, being continually raided, for apart from the tweezers, her nail scissors were ideal for pinioning all the ducklings when they were about a week old.

In the country, news of any strange event gets round remarkably quickly. If the parson's wife goes off with the verger it is soon common knowledge for miles around. Retired army officers breeding strange waterfowl seemed to come in the same category, though I suppose on reflection that Archibald sitting on the dashboard of my car on market day in Sudbury probably helped a bit to spread the news. This, as it turned out, was all to the good, for it meant that we hardly ever had to advertise birds for sale. People would come to the door, explain that they wanted to buy some ornamental waterfowl and ask to look round, just as I had done with the Colonel two years previously.

The one thing which I had to be reasonably sure about before selling any birds, was that they were proper pairs. Often, in those early days, d'Esterre would valiantly engage prospective customers in prolonged conversation on the tulip tree, the history of the house or Angus's weekly weight increases, while I was frantically shaking some unfortunate duckling up and down to see whether or not it quacked. Later I learned to sex them accurately by more intimate inspection, but we relied entirely on this Heath Robinson method during that first year. Rather surprisingly, not a single customer lodged any complaint.

That autumn, when Angus was almost walking, Ronnie presented his final bill and we moved into the house. He and the builders had done a marvellous job and we counted ourselves fortunate indeed to be living in such comfortable surroundings. There were electric shaving points in all the bedrooms (including Angus's, which seemed a little premature), ample accommodation for wine in the cellar and spacious bookshelves in the library, not to mention all the things we had actually asked to be done. For the time being ghouls and spooks were remarkable only by their absence; the three of us slept soundly at night in our beds, and the dogs likewise in their baskets. When we moved up from the cottage, one member of the family was excluded from the party. Archibald had both disgraced himself and confounded our presumptions by quacking. We toyed briefly with Lady A and Baldetta, and finally rechristened her Archibaldina, consigning her to the main pond to replace one of her aunts, a female falcated duck, who had fallen foul of a weasel.

Chapter Four

During the next two years the population both in the house and on the farm increased considerably. Eider was mated to an aristocratic golden labrador from Sussex and had a litter of eight coal black puppies; Dezzie, the dachshund, had a brief and libidinous affair with a large dog of doubtful ancestry from the village, necessitating an extremely expensive visit to the local canine abortion clinic; pheasants, a variety of new waterfowl, a nanny goat, a peacock and a trumpeter bird joined the existing menagerie; and, on 22 February 1966, d'Esterre gave birth to our daughter.

Katrina was not the only one to be christened that spring. To a peacock and an unusual, grey-winged trumpeter bird we gave the rather unimaginative names of Fluffy (later changed to Blue Boy) and Trumpy respectively; while Jack, who was currently engaged on painting the outside of the house, insisted on calling the goat Top. We were somewhat mystified over his choice of appellation until one day Jack explained the reason. Inside part of the garage, where we had constructed makeshift quarters for the goat, stood one of the heavy wooden crates which had brought our china and various ornaments back from Uganda. The original contents being fragile, d'Esterre had packed these with particular care, placing the heavier items at the bottom. I had then painted the word TOP and an arrow, hoping thereby to signify to any dim-witted stevedore the method of transportation least likely to cause damage to the contents. Jack had mistaken this for the goat's name-plate and Top she remained.

It is, we soon gathered, common practice for people to present unwanted or ailing livestock to their nearest zoo, wildlife park or bird farm. Sometimes these creatures can become a considerable embarrassment, but it is difficult to turn people away who are merely trying to do what they consider the kindest thing for the animal or bird concerned. We soon made it a rule to do the best we could for seagulls with broken wings and similar avian casualties, but to turn down politely requests for accommodation for guinea-pigs, tortoises and reticulated pythons. One spring day a woman telephoned and told me that her peahen had just started to nest when it had met a premature end at the hands, or rather teeth, of a stray dog. Would we like the only egg that the poor bird had managed to lay? That afternoon there was a knock on the door; a pot of home-made jam was offered and accepted in exchange, and I went down to the hatching shed and deposited the egg under one of my broody bantams. Twenty-four days later out popped an adorable little chick.

Partly no doubt because we spoiled him terribly and partly because he had no brothers and sisters with whom to compete for mealworms and other delicacies, Fluffy grew at such an alarming rate that when he was only eight weeks old he towered over his poor little bantam foster mother. They were a devoted couple and as soon as he was old enough to fly they would roost side by side on their perch every night. Fluffy always insisted on having a protective wing folded over him while he slept, but the larger he grew the more difficult this operation became for both of them. Eventually, when she could only envelop him by standing on tiptoe, thus invariably toppling off the perch, she admitted defeat, laid a clutch of eggs and sat on them instead. Not to be outdone that easily, Fluffy crawled in with the eggs, so that the two of them resembled one of those old-fashioned cottage loaves.

When he was about three months old, I decided it was high time he learned to fend for himself, and I caught up his long-suffering mother and put her back into the chicken house. Fluffy was prostrated with grief and cried incessantly for a whole day, and, rather to my surprise, the little bantam, who could hear his high-pitched calls of distress, was equally agitated and upset. There was nothing for it but to accept his Oedipus complex and reunite them. Fluffy was so overjoyed that he even allowed her to sit tightly on her eggs (from which of course nothing hatched as she had not been mated) while he himself sat on top of her, thus reversing the cottage loaf.

Fluffy refused to be separated from his bantam foster-mother.

While Blue Boy's (alias Fluffy's) date of birth was known with certainty and duly entered every year in my diary, together with the birthdays of my wife, my children, the dogs and any relation who might conceivably leave me any money, Trumpy's exact age was never established. I had gone to a pet shop near Cambridge to buy some Jacobin pigeons, and while I was leaning on the counter and writing out my cheque I heard an extraordinary noise behind me. I do not know whether any reader has had first-hand experience of a drunken cellist performing a *vibrato* on his lowest B. I haven't personally, but that is neither here nor there, for I imagine that cellists, like the rest of us, occasionally take part in Bacchanalian orgies and would produce sounds from their instruments not dissimilar to that which I heard. Turning round I looked accusingly at the rows of cages that faced me. Budgerigars, hamsters, kittens and a parrot all stared back morosely at me and it was clear that none of these was responsible for the noise. Then it started again, this time rising to a crescendo of volume and velocity

and culminating in a reverberating *fortissimo* hoot.

'Trumpeter bird,' announced the owner of the pet shop disinterestedly and he nodded in the direction of a cage in a dark corner. 'Forty quid, special offer this week, guv'nor.'

In the cage, surrounded by a pile of chopped tomatoes, bananas and droppings, was a creature that at first glance resembled a long-legged, small-headed, rather scruffy bantam. It was its eyes that I noticed first. They were very dark and intelligent and, as it cocked its head enquiringly at me, I observed that the feathers on its head and neck had a wonderfully velvet texture. Even in the half-light surrounding its pathetically small cage I could see that there were bright flashes of green and purple on its sooty black plumage. The wings and legs were grey. It was by no means the most beautiful bird that I had ever seen, but it certainly had the most appealing expression. I went up to the cage, put my finger through the bars and started to scratch the top of its head. At this it bent its head forward, closed it eyes and appeared to go into a swaying trance of ecstasy. Whenever I stopped caressing its head, it quickly opened its eyes and made little stringed instrument noises that were clearly intended as an encouragement for further attention. It was totally irresistible and I promptly amended the figure on my cheque. It was only when I was struggling through the door with my latest acquisitions that I realized I had not the faintest idea how to look after a trumpeter bird.

'Any old scraps will do,' the man replied to my enquiry. Trumpy and I were, I suspect, equally delighted to be out of that particular pet shop. It was a hot autumn day and I drove all the way home at a leisurely speed with the windows wide open, the pigeons in a cardboard box on the back seat and Trumpy in his little cage beside me. He clearly revelled in the sunshine and fresh air and, much to the surprise of pedestrians and other drivers, trumpeted loudly when I scratched his head every time that we drew up at traffic lights.

Trumpy's well-heralded arrival met with unqualified approval from the whole household. Even the dogs were fascinated by him. At tea that afternoon, d'Esterre put Trumpy in the place of honour in the middle of the kitchen table where he basked in all the attention. Angus scratched his head with jammy fingers through the bars and Katrina banged her spoon up and down on the tray of her high chair in a high state of glee.

After tea I rang up the local zoo for advice, and the curator told me that he recommended a diet of minced meat with a little cod-liver oil, fruit and any live insects. He also told me that I should lightly clip the feathers on one wing and give the bird the maximum possible freedom within our four-acre fox-proof enclosure. In winter he would need heated quarters. Trumpeter birds, he explained, are natives of the South American jungles where they are sometimes kept as pets by the villagers. The forest tribes often tie the young birds to the nest structure with bark or leather thongs and in this way the parent birds continue to feed them until they are old enough to fend for themselves. They are then removed and taken into the villages where they kill small snakes and act as watchdogs for the poultry.

I decided it was too late to launch Trumpy into the Daw's Hall jungle that day, so I fed him and shut him up instead in the foodshed on the farm where, tired out from all the excitement of the day, he hopped onto a corn bin, closed his eyes and went fast asleep.

The following morning, when I went to feed before breakfast, I took down with me from the house Trumpy's breakfast in a plastic dog bowl. As soon as he had eaten enough I opened the door and let him out. He was at first rather stiff and one leg seemed a little lame. It was presumably the first proper exercise that he had taken for months, or maybe years, and I noticed a little swelling on one ankle and wondered whether it was a relic of his early life in South America when perhaps he had been chained to his nest as a fledgling. If his limbs were a little rusty, his vocal chords were certainly not impaired, and after a few trial kicks from the starting block he raced off towards the main pond, trumpeting loudly. The reaction from the ducks that were in his path was such as would occur if a naked Martian were suddenly to step out of a taxi and run down the length of Bond Street. Some stood transfixed with terror, others fled screaming in all directions and only the eiders, which I had recently bought, appeared undismayed and tried to goose him *en passant*. Having successfully asserted his authority over the waterfowl, he then proceeded to the chicken run where many a matronly bird must have come close to having an apoplectic fit at the sudden sight of this apparition. After their first shock was over, however, some of the braver ones came up hesitantly to the wire netting to have a closer look at him and Trumpy responded with

Only the eiders did not flee in terror when our grey-winged trumpeter bird introduced himself to the main duck pond.

little hoots of friendship. Thereafter, he virtually ignored the ducks and was at his happiest when standing protectively by the chickens. We felt sure that this was not the first occasion in his life when he had taken on this role of poultry custodian.

Apart from the pair of eiders, there were now several other interesting additions to the waterfowl collection. I had been lucky enough to acquire an adult pair of red-breasted geese. These exquisitely beautiful birds, which are natives of eastern Europe and Russia, are notorious for their reluctance to breed in captivity. This pair, however, were somehow persuaded to abandon a policy of non-cooperation with the West and settled down happily in a capitalist society. The first spring they were with us, they nested, and two young were hatched and reared by a bantam. Several of our original geese began to nest when they were three years old and all turned out to be surprisingly easy to rear. Our only problem was in providing a sufficiently large broody hen to cover some of these big eggs. Although I had a few assorted heavyweights in the hen house, none of these seemed to go broody as readily as the Silkie bantams

and the small mongrels. Whenever we were unable to supply a broody for the goose eggs, we would let the geese hatch and rear their own young. Unlike the ducks, they were marvellous parents and we never lost a single gosling in this way.

The creatures that presented us with the most difficult problems in their infancy were the long-tailed ducks or, as they are called in America, old squaws. They are among the most northern of all birds, being found within the Arctic Circle itself, and, unique among ducks, the male has two very distinct ornamental plumages. They are extremely rare in collections and we never had an adult pair, but we did manage on two occasions to have eggs sent to us from Iceland. Knowing full well their reputation for being exceptionally hard to rear, we were, by the time the first eggs were due to hatch, well stocked with suitable delicacies for their consumption. A pail of water containing fresh-water shrimps, water fleas and all sorts of other wriggling things trapped by the shrimping nets stood in a cool corner of the food-shed. Sadly, only two eggs out of a dozen hatched. When the ducklings were dry we carefully carried them and their bantam foster-mother into an outside brooder, where a veritable gourmet's dream awaited them. The only gourmets present, however, were the broody hen and Trumpy. Doubtless anxious to celebrate in good style the end of her four weeks in solitary confinement on a diet of wheat and water, the broody promptly consumed every *bonne bouche* there was. Trumpy, always anxious to come and inspect any new arrivals on the farm, jumped on top of the wire frame of the brooder, hooted loudly and added his contribution to the water bowl. When I pushed him off he landed in the pail that was standing nearby containing our gastronomic reserves. Much to his delight the pail tipped over and he succeeded in consuming most of the contents before we could rescue them. While all this commotion was going on the two ducklings were frantically trying to jump up and escape. One died that evening and the other three days later. The next year, when we succeeded in hatching five long-tailed ducklings, I took the double precaution of locking Trumpy up in the 'hospital' for the first few days and using an infra-red lamp rather than a hen to provide warmth for the babies. In this way we succeeded in rearing two young long-tailed ducklings. I was so proud of these two birds that they were christened Sir Percival and Lady Longtail.

Many of our original ducks became prolific layers in their second and third years and, although a high percentage of eggs turned out to be infertile, we reared large numbers of ducklings. Fertility among the burping and whistle-sneezing wood ducks was especially disappointing and I soon realized that this was one of many aspects of our new life about which I was still extremely ignorant. July and August were always fiendish months when the population on the farm doubled or trebled in size, but by Christmas every year we managed to find homes for almost all the young stock. Barbarossa and Mrs Barbarossa had been joined by two further pairs of red-crested pochards and the offspring from these were particularly popular with our customers. All the young male Cape teal that we reared seemed to have inherited their father's characteristics, while Mrs Cocky regularly had the most consistent fertility of all our ducks. Although these young teal were both charming and easy to rear, there was more than one comment from new owners on the ferocious, over-sexed behaviour exhibited by the males. After a couple of years of this, I decided it was only fair to warn people in advance that Cockies were best kept in isolation from other ducks. Among the other birds that nested were the falcated ducks and cereopsis geese. Archibaldina was a loyal wife to the falcated drake to whom she was paired and, rather hurtfully, had fallen completely out of love* with me. It was hard to realize that this was the same little bird that only two years before had stood peeping plaintively for me outside the loo in the cottage. In contrast, the volatile temperament of Henry, the cereopsis gander, remained totally unchanged. On one occasion he succeeded in jumping over his fence and almost killing Eider, the labrador. Their second year with us was a repeat performance of the first. All their eggs were addled, only this time I managed, with the aid of a friend, to remove their rotten eggs without them exploding. In their third year Henrietta finally succeeded in hatching a solitary gosling. Fate, however, obviously decreed that this was an endangered species to which Daw's Hall Wildfowl Farm was to make a negative contribution. When it was about a month old and progressing well, it somehow succeeded in committing suicide by hanging itself in the forked base of the holly tree. Henrietta tried to embark on a second clutch but died from

*Ethnologists term this behaviour 'imprinting'.

egg peritonitis. Whipsnade Zoo were, at the time, short of a gander, and the last I heard of Henry was that he was the scourge of all the zoo attendants and the father of squadrons of young cereopsis.

One winter's day, at a comparatively slack period on the farm, we drove to a place in Bedfordshire where there was a well-known collection of ornamental pheasants that was open to the public. The children came too: Katrina adored travelling in the car, while Angus from a very early age had begun to take an intelligent interest in wildlife. We saw all sorts of exotic pheasants, including many that I had never heard of before, but it was the golden pheasants, some of which were wandering freely around the garden, that impressed us most. The hens were drab little birds, not unlike the females of the well-known breeds of game pheasant, but the plumage of the cock birds must surely have rivalled even Jacob's coat of many colours. There were golds, scarlets, blues and greens and, as they pirouetted and displayed to their wives and to each other, they fanned out the orange and black ruffs round their necks. It was not only their marvellous grace and beauty that appealed to us. We also discovered that, for a price only slightly more than one had to pay the butcher for a brace of pheasants for the table, we could actually buy a pair of live golden pheasants for the farm. As usual, I got hopelessly carried away in my enthusiasm and we came away with three pairs, that leapt around like jumping beans in their cardboard boxes in the car, much to the amusement of the children, particularly when one box landed in Katrina's lap.

When we got home, I lightly clipped one wing on each bird and let them loose in the little wood round the main pond. They hopped up to roost every evening in a big holly bush close to the gate and found a mass of natural food during the daytime in the hedgerows. Trumpy would now spend part of the day with them, particularly if he thought there was any likelihood of delicious morsels being unearthed from beneath the dead leaves. While he was singularly useless at finding food for himself, he was an arch demon at grabbing everybody else's dinner just as they were about to eat it. One of his favourite pastimes was to come into the garden when we were digging in the flower beds and stand by eagerly for any tidbits to appear. Every time a worm came to the surface he would pounce on it with a loud trumpeting call, much to the dismay of a tame robin and Blue Boy, who had previously considered this their preserve.

Trumpy posed no problems when the weather was warm, but we had to be careful to provide him with extra heat in the winter. Although we kept a large flock of bantams for hatching the waterfowl eggs, we had begun to change over to infra-red lamps for rearing the ducklings, as this more idle method constituted a considerable saving in time and labour. These lamps also came in very handy during cold spells for giving extra heat to any sick birds, to ducks from more tropical regions and particularly to Trumpy. I made it a firm rule every day from December to the end of March to catch him up each afternoon, give him his minced meat and fruit and then shut him up for the night. At first, this operation used to go off very smoothly. Trumpy invariably knew when it was time for his tea and would be waiting for me in his winter quarters, the door of which I used to leave open for him. After a while, however, he became tired of this routine and decided that freedom, risk of frostbite and exhilarating games were far more fun. Fun it doubtless was for him, but I cannot admit to sharing his enjoyment when, at the end of a long and tiring day, with darkness rapidly descending and a pile of paper-work awaiting me in the house, I had to pander to his wishes and play hide-and-seek and grandmother's footsteps with him in the wood. For the first few days I quite enjoyed these games, for he always chose the same hiding place, behind a big oak tree close to the pond, and all I had to do was to creep up quietly and pounce. It was not long, however, before he developed new and perfectly infuriating tactics. First, he would conceal himself, always in a different place, while I would systematically search through the undergrowth and behind all the trees, getting crosser and crosser all the time. Then, if I was getting warm or had managed to spot him, he would quickly run away and hide in a new place. Off I would set, red in the face, and each time I got near him again he would peer cheekily from behind a tree, trumpet loudly and gallop off to the next hiding place.

One day, after I had spent about an hour looking for him, I was convinced he must have died or disappeared for good. It was getting dark and d'Esterre and I were already late for an evening of bridge with some friends. Just as I was about to abandon the search, I noticed what I took to be a dead moorhen floating face downwards in the pond. On looking closer, I saw to my horror that it was Trumpy. Grabbing a long stick, I managed with difficulty to steer him to the bank and fish him out. He was limp and appeared quite lifeless and I dreaded having to break the news to the family who would, I knew, be heartbroken. To make absolutely sure, I held his cold, damp little body close to my ear and listened. There was just the faintest sound of life. I rushed up to the house at top speed, switched the oven on as low as possible and put the bedraggled remains of our grey-winged trumpeter bird in the roasting pan normally reserved for the Sunday joint. That evening the standard of my bridge was abysmal. Twice, entirely through my lack of concentration, we went three down doubled and, in the final hand, when I should have made a grand slam, one miserable little trump that I had forgotten took the last trick. I drove home at breakneck speed, to the accompaniment of a well-deserved ticking off from d'Esterre. Parking the car outside the back door, I ran into the kitchen, switched on the light and there was Trumpy jumping up and down in the roasting pan, scolding us in no uncertain terms for having abandoned him in his hour of need. His recovery was quite remarkable, but for the rest of the winter I took no further chances and he spent both day and night firmly locked up in one of the rearing pens.

When spring came and Trumpy had resumed his customary stance outside the hen run, the three pairs of golden pheasants took up separate territories around the main pond and started to nest. Though I watched the hen birds very carefully, not once during their three weeks of incubation did I see any of them come off their eggs. Whether their sole sustenance during this period was moisture from the dew, or whether the cock birds brought food to them, I do not know. Maybe they slipped off for brief periods when I was not about, but intuition told me otherwise. It is a strange fact that the nest in the natural haunts of this most common of all ornamental pheasants, which has been famous in Chinese art and literature for many centuries, has yet to be described.

Collections and hobbies usually begin with a surge of enthusiasm, and in many instances the enthusiasm wanes surprisingly quickly. The fifteen year old boy, who thinks, for instance, that butterfly collecting is a cissy pastime, forgets the fanatical ardour that he may have applied to this selfsame hobby only a few years earlier. At Daw's Hall Wildfowl Farm we had brief and unsuccessful flirtations with strange breeds of pigeons, old-fashioned poultry and sheep. But now, writing thirteen years after we first bought the farm, it is clear that only the waterfowl and pheasants have advanced relentlessly from strength to strength. From golden pheasants, we progressed to silvers; then to the Lady Amherst, Reeves, Swinhoe's and Elliot's. What horrified us most, and certainly contributed in no small way to our determination to keep and breed these birds successfully, was the discovery that approximately one third of all the known forms of pheasants were currently endangered in the wild.

Many people in Britain are aware of only one type of pheasant, the bird that struts around stubble fields and hedgerows in the autumn and falls to knickerbockered gentry in the winter. It is commonly assumed that Britain has always had its population of pheasants, but this is not so. The Chinese ringneck, melanistic, Mongolian and others all originally came from Eastern Europe and Asia and were believed to have been first imported to this country by the Romans. Their use then was strictly cullinary and they provided an alternative to wild boar, venison or oyster's on the rich man's table. Some succeeded in evading this fate by escaping into the wild, and gradually they began to populate the countryside. These were the same species of bird that Aeschylus and the Greeks had found living along the river Phasis and called the birds of Colchis, from which their Latin name of *phasianus colchicus* is derived. Apart from these game pheasants there are lesser known varieties distributed throughout Asia and one, the Congo peacock, was discovered only this century living in the heart of Africa. Altogether, there are approximately one hundred and fifty different forms known to science, ranging from the magnificent argus pheasant that is found in tropical jungles to the little partridge-like blood pheasant from high altitudes in the Himalayas and China. Sadly for them, all pheasants are delicious to eat and most of the males have wonderful plumages that are as coveted as headpieces by savage tribes in Borneo as they are for more sophisticated headwear in London, Paris and New York. These two factors, coupled with the ever-increasing destruction of much of their natural habitat, have caused many of them to become threatened with extinction.

Building aviaries was a time-consuming job, and if the finished article was to look at all presentable, a basic knowledge of carpentry was essential. While I would certainly have won prizes for mixing and barrowing cement, hoeing round Christmas trees or dropping maggots into the mouths of recalcitrant ducklings, the standard of my carpentry was, frankly, hopeless.

D'Esterre and I had decided, shortly after moving into the house, that the time had come to employ a full-time man, who would live in the cottage and work on the farm.

With more than thirty acres of land, a large garden and an ever-increasing menagerie, there was ample work for ten lusty Irish navvies for three hundred and sixty five days every year. In fact, we employed three men, none of them Irish and none simultaneously. All shall be nameless and all, in varying ways, failed to come up to our expectations. The first had an uncontrollable fear of chickens and only admitted after he had started work that he had a gammy leg; the second kept potatoes and rats in the spare bedroom at the cottage and finally chose a time when I was flat on my back with a slipped disc to vanish into a mental home; the third went to gaol. Despite their minor shortcomings, and the necessity for strict supervision, they took a lot of the burden off my shoulders. It meant, moreover, that we could get away rather more frequently, though never with complete peace of mind. The casualty list when we were away was always distressingly high and on one of these occasions Sir Percival and Lady Longtail mysteriously disappeared.

On the credit side, the garden gradually became less of a jungle, Top the goat did sterling work reducing the nettles and brambles in the orchard, the weeds in the Christmas tree field could now be controlled with a rotovator and a lot of constructional work was done on the farm. Pheasant aviaries started to take shape and the ponds themselves at last began to look less like barren craters on the moon. On the land I had recently acquired, we installed a pump beside a little stream that ran into the river, and this increased considerably the flow of water through the three ponds. Even the bottom pond kept its level well and was stocked with new varieties of waterfowl. One crop that sadly never reappeared was the poppies. There must have been some association between them and their normal companion crop of corn, for they declined to grow among our young pine trees.

Early in 1968 we advertised once again for a man to join me on the farm. Apart from two old age pensioners and a West Indian schoolboy, there were two applicants, both of whom contacted me by telephone. The first was the son of a Welsh gamekeeper, the second clearly came from further afield. He spoke with a deep gutteral accent that I took to be German, announced his name, which I failed to catch, and informed me that he worked in a restaurant in Brentwood. None of these things seemed in any way to qualify him particularly for the work on my farm, so we settled, blind, for the Welshman, and told our gutteral enquirer that we were sadly unable to offer him any employment. Two days later the gamekeeper's son sent me a telegram: his father had died suddenly, he himself had to take over his father's work and he much regretted that he could not come to us. There was nothing for it but to have a look at the restaurateur and hope he would be suitable. I arranged for him to come for an interview the following Sunday.

It was a warm afternoon in spring when sharp at three o'clock a huge white jaguar pulled up outside the house. Out stepped an extremely attractive blonde with a small baby in her arms, followed by a bearded giant, whose apparel was quite remarkable. Apart from a vast cigar, still with the band on, between hiss teeth, and the briefest pair of bathing trunks I had ever seen, he was naked down to his feet. These were inserted into an outsize pair of Dutch clogs.

'Major Grahm?' he enquired and no sooner had I admitted to my identity than my hand was clasped in a vice-like grip. 'I am Cornelius Stapel,' — it rhymed with carpel — 'and this is my wife Hedwig and our daughter Monique.' D'Esterre shook hands with the blonde but, after glancing sympathetically at the remains of my right hand, bowed politely to the giant.

We set off on a tour of inspection, first to the cottage, which obviously met with their approval, particularly since he could stand in every room without knocking his head on the beams, and then to see the birds. It was clear from the comments that he made as we strolled along together that he was in his element. He told me that when he had lived in Holland he had kept various breeds of waterfowl of his own. He had no trouble in identifying the ducks and geese that we kept, only in giving the correct English names. Hedwig, his wife, was beautiful, vivacious and evidently very talented. A successful career as a fashion model had first brought her to this country about ten years previously and she had subsequently travelled extensively on assignments in Europe and North Africa. After her first marriage, from which she had a young son called Eric, had broken down, she had worked as a free-lance journalist and then had thrown herself in at the deep end of the catering business by buying the restaurant in Brentwood. There she had met Cornelius, who was at that time working as the representative of a Dutch bulb firm. They had been married a year.

I liked them both enormously and felt instinctively that he would be a wonderful person to work with, but I was very concerned that being the duck-man of Daw's Hall could well be a retrograde step in his career. Moreover, I could not quite see Hedwig adjusting to a life of gumboots and isolation in our aptly named Pitmire Lane Cottage, which was a hundred yards down one of the muddiest farm tracks in East Anglia and far better suited to a jeep than to a jaguar.

Over tea I explained carefully to both of them that it was hardly the most lucrative career open to them, and advised them to think it over very carefully before committing themselves. We had not long to wait for an answer, for he telephoned later that night to confirm that he wanted the job. D'Esterre and I were delighted and we arranged to go and have supper in their restaurant the following evening, to finalize the arrangements.

The only goldfish out of water that I had ever seen had been many years before, when my first pet had expired at my feet on the nursery floor. Goldie's expression had remained vivid in my mind and it was not dissimilar to that of Cornelius Stapel as, draped in a tiny apron, he stood forlornly gazing into space through the window of the restaurant in Brentwood. When he saw us his face brightened perceptibly. 'Ah, good evening. Vot vould you like to dreenk?' he enquired, a huge cigar once again clenched firmly between his teeth. We settled for two dry martinis, followed by *weiner schnitzel* and lager beer, and then his wife appeared from the kitchen looking more like a Hartnell mannequin than a cook. The spotlessness of the establishment was very noticeable; dolls in Dutch national costume and pictures of windmills festooned the walls, while a gramophone wafted the soft strains of *Tulips from Amsterdam*. While d'Esterre and I and a few other customers were eating our meals, Cornelius hovered in the background, polishing glasses, taking orders and trying without much success to play the part of the perfect, invisible waiter. His six foot eight inch frame would have been better fitted for the helm of a Viking long-boat than for transporting *pâté maison* to the tables and dropping stuffed olives into cocktail glasses. The clogs had been replaced by huge, hand-made leather slippers and I wondered momentarily how on earth he would manage for gumboots. By the time we got to the coffee, the restaurant had cleared and we all had a chance to sit down together over a drink and discuss plans for their arrival in two weeks time. They had found a buyer for the restaurant and had already booked a removal firm to bring their possessions to Lamarsh. The only problem appeared to be whether their Brobdingnagian bed would ever get into the cottage, let alone up the stairs and into their bedroom.

Not only did the bed take up residence, carried in single-handed by Cornelius while the wilting removal men watched in amazement, but within a few days the cottage had had a complete face-lift. The rooms were scrubbed, carpets laid and piles of junk from the previous three incumbents removed and buried. The cottage garden, neglected for years, was dug and sown with neat rows of vegetables and flowers and then, having sorted out his own property, he turned his attention and bulging biceps to mine. We noticed that his wife's name was invariably shortened to Hedy, while she always referred to him as Case, or so it sounded to us. All of us were soon on Christian name terms, which was much easier all round, but his abbreviation puzzled us somewhat. One morning, I wanted to get a message to him, as we were going up to London for the day, so I left an envelope marked 'Case' just inside the back door. When we got back, I found a note for me which read: 'Dear Iain, I am not a suitcase. Cees'.

Spurred on by Cees's enthusiasm and tremendous energy, we concocted all sorts of new and exciting ideas for the farm and the garden and, with me alternating between plumber's mate, carpenter's assistant and general dog's body, the whole place gradually began to be transformed. Like many of his fellow-countrymen, Cees was in his element with water, and one of the first things to which he turned his attention were the dams along the streams leading down to the main pond. Foreign oaths were hurled on the heads of Ronnie's builders, who had advised me over the initial construction, and his herculean shoulders smashed their puny efforts to smithereens and proper Dutch dams took their place. When these were finished, we turned our attention to the pheasant aviaries. The dozen or so existing ones were modified and improved and new, palatial housing was put up for tropical varieties.

The majority of pheasants have no problems in withstanding the rigours of an English winter, but there are some that must be given protection from frost. This can be provided in a variety of ways, and we soon discovered that underfloor heating was the most effective. This we installed by laying electric heating cables in the concrete floors of the covered parts of the aviaries. It was an instant success and enabled us to keep new and exciting breeds, like firebacks and peacock pheasants. The latter, as their name implies, have wonderful irridescent 'eyes' (or ocelli) on parts of their plumage and resemble miniature, bantam-size peafowl. Blue Boy, our only true peacock, had been eventually persuaded to part from his little foster-mother by our acquiring a wife for him. By the time he was three years old, he had grown a magnificent train and was the proud father of six enchanting offspring. We also acquired a pair of pure white peafowl. White Boy looked ravishingly beautiful when the weather was dry but, if it was damp and muddy underfoot, his apparel resembled that of the housewife on a television commercial who has failed to use the correct brand of detergent.

One of the most important contributions that Cees made was to our rearing system. My early technique of allowing broody hens to rear little families of ducklings, pheasants and goslings in movable arcs outside, while perfectly effective for small numbers of the easier ornamental breeds, was both time-consuming and open to risk from infection. The arcs had regularly to be moved onto fresh ground and even then we found that many of our rare breeds were by no means as resistant to diseases as are mallard and ordinary game pheasants. Furthermore, we had to be permanently watchful for changes in the weather. On hot summer days extra shade had to be given and, whenever the heavens opened, one of us had to rush out and put the removable polythene roofs on all the arcs. Cees turned one of the old apple storage sheds on the farm into a series of small indoor rearing pens, each heated by an infra-red lamp and each thoroughly disinfected after each family of young birds had passed through this stage.

We continued to use a broody for most of the pheasants, though there was always a lamp in case of emergencies, and lamps instead of hens were used invariably for the ducklings. Pheasants, even at an early age, are extremely pugnacious creatures and will quickly set upon and often kill other members of their own family. While young pheasants in a confined space will almost always react in this way to others of their kind that were not actually hatched with them, ducklings by contrast are exceptionally benevolent and forbearing towards other ducklings. Our new system with them, therefore, was to allow the broodies to sit on the eggs until they were chipped, then to put the eggs into an incubator for hatching. The long suffering bantams were then given a second clutch to sit on and the ducklings were transferred to an indoor rearing pen as soon as they were ready to come out of the incubator. The older ducklings seemed to enjoy mothering the babies and teaching them to feed and one pen would hold up to twenty or thirty young birds. When they were about three weeks old and depending on the weather, both pheasants and waterfowl were moved outside to more spacious and unheated rearing quarters. For the ducklings and goslings this would be the first time that they would be allowed to have a swim. It is not always realized that, in the wild, the mother duck, while brooding her young, transfers some of her own waterproofing to them so that they are well equipped to take to the water very soon after birth. Artificial rearing methods cannot compete with nature in this way, and many people have discovered to their surprise that a little pair of webbed feet is not the only requisite for an embryonic Olympic swimmer.

Shortly after Cees's arrival, he announced that his own menagerie at the cottage, which already consisted of a few chickens and Dutch call ducks, was going to be increased by the arrival of a pair of African pygmy goats. Paul and Paula came from a zoo in the north of England and travelled by train to Colchester station, where Cees and I collected them in my shooting-brake. They were enchanting little animals, less than half the size of any goats that I had previously seen, and the breed apparently originated from Nigeria. They settled happily into the little paddock behind the cottage and Paul's strong odour was soon pervading the whole farm. In due course a daughter, Paulette, was born to them, who was smaller at birth than some of the Stapels' chickens. Cees told me that the pygmies had only one serious shortcoming in his eyes. Unlike other domesticated goats, they could not be milked which, he explained, was extremely unfortunate since he himself had a particular *penchant* for goats' milk. More than once he gazed hungrily at Top's udder and suggested that I should get her a mate.

While Paul, Paula and Paulette were gambolling happily in

their enclosure at the recently renamed Rosabella Cottage, Top continued her rather lonely existence some two hundred yards away in the orchard behind Daw's Hall. Each morning she was tethered to a fresh piece of ground and, at the end of the day, after the birds had been fed, she would be led back to the garage where she would spend the night. She clearly thrived on her diet of coarse grass, weeds and brambles, and I remember d'Esterre remarking one day on her middle-age spread.

One afternoon, when I went up as usual to collect Top, I saw to my amazement that instead of one goat we had two. A little kid was happily nuzzling her udder. How this apparently immaculate conception had occurred was a mystery. So far as I knew, there were no stray billy goats rampaging through the local countryside, nor was Paul likely to have had the opportunity, let alone the capability of committing any such felony. It would have been as improbable a mating as that between a dachshund and an alsation. I went off to find Cees and told him what had happened.

'Oh, zat is very strange, but I shall much enjoy all zis beautiful goat's milk,' was his only comment, as he sucked innocently on his pipe.

'But Cees, you must have some idea how this could have happened,' I persisted.

He regarded me quizzically for a moment or two before announcing blandly: 'I theenk maybe ze sparrows carry ze seed.'

After a home had been found for the young billy, Cees sat every morning and evening on an upturned bucket in the garage and with his great big hands extracted the milk. Sometimes he could not even wait to get down to the cottage before sampling the ambrosial liquid, and more than once he emerged from Top's stable with milk dripping from his beard and a rapturous expression on his face. It was a long time before he finally admitted to me that gluttony had in fact got the better of him and that he, Paul and a tea-chest had, between them, been responsible for the perpetration of this villainous deed.

Chapter Five

The year 1968 was concluded on a sad note. D'Esterre and I separated shortly before Christmas and she and the children moved to London.

There were many occasions during the next three years when, sitting alone in the house late at night, I wondered whether our resident ghost or ghosts would pay me a visit. Branches from the lime trees outside the windows of the old part of the house creaked and rustled in the wind and starlings nested noisily in the huge Tudor chimney, but never at night did I hear or see anything unusual. Nevertheless, one or two of the older residents of the village told me that they could not understand how I could sleep in the haunted house on my own. I did, however, hear the ghost dog on two or three occasions, but always during the day. It happened at most unlikely times — once when I was making a telephone call after breakfast — and though I never felt frightened or disturbed in any way, I had not the slightest doubt that these sounds were not attributable to any natural causes. Eider, my labrador, was asleep under my desk on one occasion when I heard the familiar noise of our paranormal canine resident just outside the library. Quickly waking her, I ran with her to the door and into the back passage from where the noise was coming. Hoping that she would react in an appropriate, hackle-raising fashion, I was sadly disappointed. The noise stopped instantly and she just stood there wagging her tail. Another incident will always remain crystal-clear in my mind. I had collected Mrs Newman, the daily cleaning lady, from the neighbouring village as usual at nine o'clock in the morning, had deposited her at the house and had gone onto the farm to see Cees. About half an hour later I came back to the house to have a cup of coffee and happened to glance up towards the top of the house just before coming in through the back door. There, in an attic window, I saw a woman's face. It was only for a split second and I merely thought it strange that Mrs Newman should have gone into the attic, which was a part of the house that was never used. I was startled, however, when I found her sitting down to her regular cuppa in the kitchen. I rushed up the two flights of stairs and into the attic, but there was nothing whatever to see.

Shortly after this, something very different occurred. At the time, it made me seriously wonder whether I ought not to go and have a confidential talk with my doctor. It was a Sunday afternoon and I strolled down to the vegetable garden to cut some asparagus for my supper. As I rounded the corner of the garden wall an enormous bird flew out from a nearby oak tree and over the house where it disappeared from view. Now, even the best ornithologists are not always infallible in recognizing the difference between, for example, marsh tits and willow tits, but there are some birds which are quite unmistakable. One of these is the golden eagle and this was the bird that I saw at a range of less than fifty feet flying leisurely over my garden on the borders of Suffolk and Essex.

It was in fact my doctor, himself a very keen bird-watcher, who got in touch with me. He too had seen this apparition in his garden and had noticed a small paragraph in the local paper describing how a tame eagle had escaped from its owner's premises near Ipswich. Though I never saw it again, we lost two garganey teal from the island pond the next day. Whether the eagle succumbed to an astonished East Anglian gamekeeper, or whether it winged its way northwards to a more salubrious area, we never discovered.

Apart from sales of birds, the farm was beginning to produce two other sources of income. The Christmas trees had duly responded to the regular cultivations and were growing steadily at the rate of about a foot a year. After three years some of them had reached a marketable size. Our first customers were the local shops, all of whom insisted that the trees be dug, not sawn, and that we refrained from boiling the roots. During the last week of November and the first week in December Cees and I would advance upon the field each day armed with spades, binder twine and measuring sticks. Cees, as usual, took on the skilled work of severing the main roots and lifting the trees, coping with close on a hundred every hour. My contribution was far less spectacular and consisted of

A golden eagle was an unexpected visitor to Daw's Hall.

cleaning the roots, dragging the trees to a central collecting base, grading them and tying them into bundles of five. Our Christmas tree harvest always seemed to coincide with a period of frost, snow and biting east winds. How people could envisage anyone in these conditions prolonging their agony by sedulously dipping the roots of every tree into a cauldron of boiling water was something I could never understand. It is, of course, the extremes of temperature, from frosted fields to stuffy, overheated shops and living rooms, that almost invariably put paid to a Christmas tree's chances of surviving.

Our second additional source of revenue from the farm was also seasonal. For two or three years we had been far too charitable to hosts of strangers who drove up to the house, often at the most inconvenient moments, and asked to be allowed to see the birds.

74

While I had made it a firm rule never to allow visitors during the breeding season, when the birds were particularly vulnerable to the slightest disturbance, I had always tried to accommodate random callers at other times of the year. Although the World Wildlife Fund collecting box that stood by the gate benefited considerably from generous contributions from these visitors, all I received were perpetual requests to picnic on the lawn and enquiries as to the location of the toilets. Cees and I decided the time had come to adopt a more mercenary attitude and for Daw's Hall to open officially to the public.

Every Saturday and Sunday afternoon in August and September, with various friends sitting with the cash box outside the main gate, three guides (Cees, Hedy and myself) would take it in turn to conduct groups of people round the birds. Children were admitted at half the price of adults, though we often had cause to regret that the scale was not reversed. Little fingers, when not discarding toffee papers, would attempt to fiddle with the hook-and-eye fasteners to the pheasant aviaries, while youthful enthusiasm often lent wings to tiny feet in the waterfowl enclosures.

It was never my intention for the farm to be laid out like a zoo and for the public to wander at will; so the guides were essential to shepherd the groups in an orderly manner, to point out the various species of birds and animals, and to answer questions and explain the importance of captive breeding. An ever increasing number of pheasants are becoming threatened with extinction in the wild, so maintaining a sound stock in captivity is becoming more vital all the time. Neither we nor the birds, with a few notable exceptions, enjoyed these weekend invasions, but it was a remunerative experience and one not devoid of its lighter moments.

Two birds that revelled in mass adulation were Blue Boy and Trumpy. The latter in particular saw to it that the public had value for their money. Rattling the small change in the cash box would bring him running up to the gate where each party of visitors assembled before setting off on their tour. If anyone had failed — and few had — to remark on the pint-size, ostrich-shaped bird that was asking for its head to be scratched through the wire netting, Trumpy would quickly go into his drunken cellist routine. This instantly produced the desired effect, and once the gates were open Trumpy would rush from one party to another, checking solicitously that everyone was having a happy time and rendering any form of serious human commentary or discussion virtually impossible. His PR work was outstanding and his fame spread far and wide. I remember one man remarking, as he walked through the gate towards the ducks on the main pond, 'I didn't realize you kept *other birds* too.'

The attitude of most of our visitors to the many different varieties of birds on view was interesting. The most popular creatures were those that they could laugh at, or ones with particularly gaudy plumages. Had we kept nothing but trumpeter birds, golden pheasants, araucanas and silkie bantams, our attendance figures would no doubt have rivalled those of Woburn and Longleat. The araucanas were great favourites since, unlike all other breeds of poultry, they lay blue or green eggs. Other creatures that were much admired were Cees's pygmy goats and Indian runner ducks. The least popular members of our menagerie were the less colourful pheasants. On one occasion I was standing with a group of people beside an aviary containing one of our rarest pairs and a woman suddenly enquired 'Don't they need any water?' Thinking I must have forgotten to fill up their small plastic bowl, I looked on the floor of the aviary and saw that it contained at least half a pint of clean water. Somewhat mystified, I pointed this out to the woman, who then announced rather angrily that she considered it totally insufficient space 'for the poor little birds to swim in.' On my politely explaining that pheasants did not normally swim, she retorted, 'Oh, I'm ever so sorry, I thought they were ducks.' Another time I was showing a pair of Koklass pheasants to a party of visitors. 'These birds are Koklass,' I announced, 'and they are among the most difficult of all pheasants to breed in captivity.'

'Hardly surprisin' if 'e 'asn't got a flippin' cock,' came the wry comment from one wag in the party.

When winter came, Trumpy became increasingly unhappy at spending his time in the isolation of the heated rearing quarters on the farm, so I decided to bring him into the house where he quickly made himself at home on top of the central heating boiler and amused himself by catching mice in the cellar. He was always quick to hear voices in the house and invariably announced his presence with loud hoots of excitement. When friends came to dinner, Trumpy and the port would be placed on the table simultaneously. Thereafter nothing was safe. Ear-rings, spectacles and cigarette lighters were as vulnerable to his rapacious bill as were liqueurs and evening dresses to the opposite end of his anatomy. When Angus and Katrina came and stayed with a nanny for part of the holidays, they and Trumpy had a particularly happy time together in the playroom. One of his favourite games was to play hide-and-seek with various toys of theirs behind the curtains.

After three happy and eventful years at Daw's Hall, Trumpy suffered a heart attack and died. His remains are buried under the tall cedar tree overlooking the main pond.

Creatures that have fascinated me since childhood are bees, and when our neighbouring farmer planted a large acreage of beans just across our boundary, it seemed too good an opportunity to miss. I bought an empty hive in the local market and placed an order for a colony with a firm of apiarists. A few weeks later a very worried official from British Railways at Colcheser station telephoned and asked me to remove a box of bees from the parcels office as swiftly as possible. I told him I would be there in half an hour's time and assured him that they were quite safe so long as they remained in their box. 'Yeh, but that's just wot I'm worried about, guv,' he replied in obvious distress. 'Them bleeders are buzzin' like crazy and I knows it's just a matter of minutes before they bite their way out.' On arrival at the station I found the clerk had left nothing to chance and had locked himself up in his office adjoining the parcels shed. It took me a long time to persuade the fellow to come out and allow me to sign the receipt for them. 'Blimey,' he said as I eventually climbed into the car with the box still intact, 'I've had monkeys, cats, tropical fish and even a skunk through this shed, but this consignment takes the bleedin' biscuit.'

Back home, I carried the box up to the top of the orchard, where I had already set up the hive, and placed it in a shady corner until later in the afternoon when I hoped the occupants would be less active. Then, resembling an explorer of outer space in my voluminous white bee-suit, veil and gloves, I gingerly opened the box and lifted the frames into the hive. Most of the bees were clustered together on these frames and transferring them to their new abode was consequently a surprisingly simple operation. Quite a number, however, were sitting forlornly at the bottom of the box, so I left their travelling case close to the hive entrance and they soon joined up with their companions. The queen I never saw, but presumed that she was somewhere among the main throng. I did, however, notice a number of portly drones. These males would, I knew, lead an enviable and indolent existence until the autumn, when they would be unceremoniously evicted from the hive and left to die of cold and starvation.

I was putting the roof back on the hive and congratulating myself on the success of the operation when suddenly my hand slipped. In trying to regain my balance I lurched forward and fell on top of the hive with a sickening thud. All hell broke loose. Within seconds I was surrounded by a vast and infuriated horde of bees who pursued me all the way back to the house. My beginner's manual had stressed the importance of slow, calculated movements in handling these creatures. I had broken the cardinal rule of beekeeping and was extremely lucky to have escaped intact.

The following morning, I tiptoed up to the colony in some trepidation. It was a sunny day and the bees were busy foraging for nectar and pollen, and the peaceful humming that emanated from the hive was a pleasant contrast to the angry noise of the previous afternoon. Every two or three weeks during the summer, I made a careful inspection of the interior of their home, adding extra supers for the storage of honey, pinching out queen cells and watching the progress of the colony. It was a fascinating experience and I never ceased to marvel at the high degree of discipline and organization within the hive, a salutary lesson indeed to the human race.

There are, I know, beekeepers who rush up to tell their bees that the bank rate has just been increased, or that the stock market has taken a dive, and confide in them the innermost secrets of their private lives. Whether these snippets of information interest or amuse the bees, no-one has yet determined. I did, however, soon discover that it does pay to talk to the bees, if only to say 'Mind you don't sting me today, you little perishers,' as the beekeeper's voice undoubtedly gives them a little advance warning of his presence.

Apart from sudden movements and ham-fisted handling of the hive, bees are reputed to respond violently to the smell of BO, hair oil and after-shave lotion. That summer I witnessed an example of their strong aversion to such smells. Cees, who soon began to share my fascination for the bees and whose predilection for honey was almost as strong as for goat's milk, was helping me to take our first crop. The bees were resenting the removal of the fruits of their labours and there was a cloud of angry insects all round the hive.

Desite our protective clothing, we had already suffered more than one sting apiece. In the middle of the operation, I heard a voice shouting to us from the area of the drive. Looking up, we saw a man with a very anxious face and hair liberally plastered with oil holding a couple of samples of fire extinguishers. Quite undeterred by the somewhat unusual position and activities of his audience, he proceeded, from a range of about thirty yards, to embark on his well-rehearsed patter of salesmanship. Had we seen his latest model ... ? Did we realize the enormous discounts available for cash purchases ... ?

'For God's sake, get back into your car,' I yelled. 'There's an extremely angry lot of bees around here and I don't want you to get stung. Leave your card inside the back door.'

Either he failed to hear me, or else the valour and persistence of this particular travelling salesman was such as wins a posthumous Victoria Cross in times of war. Several bees started to attack him, but still the eulogies on the merits of the fire extinguishers continued. His face was now the colour of his merchandise and occasionally one arm would try to swat a bee from his well-groomed hair. The panegyrics, however persisted and I realised that either I would have to cough up fifteen pounds for a fire extinguisher for which I had not the slightest requirement, or we should have a casualty in urgent need of an antihistamine injection. 'All right, I'll buy one,' I shouted to him. 'Drop it off when you're next in this area.'

The crop that summer was a little over forty pounds of honey, and the following year Cees and I decided to increase our stocks. I was on the point of ordering another colony when a neighbour telephoned to say that there was a swarm flying around her garden. I rushed up to our original hive and discovered that their numbers had become seriously depleted. A new queen must have hatched and one of the two monarchs had eloped with her retinue. In the neighbouring garden I watched as they circled round the house and then saw to my horror that they were starting to cluster high up in an oak tree, almost a hundred foot from the ground. I quickly went back to the farm for Cees, protective clothing and some mountaineering equipment.

Since Cees had an uncontrollable fear of heights, we both knew in advance who was going to be the fall guy in this particular exploit. With a long rope tied round my waist, I managed without

79

too much difficulty to climb up to within reach of the swarm. Cees then tied the other end of the rope to the travelling box in which the original colony came and I hauled it up to where I was precariously perched, about three foot below the swarm which was almost as large as a football.

More often than not bees will select a site within easy reach of *terra firma* and, with both one's legs solidly on the ground and both arms free to shake them into a box or skep, the taking of a swarm is a straightforward operation. Only madmen pursue them up church steeples and mature oak trees, and Cees's wry comment, 'Eef you are going to fall, please shout first so that I can get out of ze vay,' was hardly calculated to improve the state of my morale. I knew the moment of truth would come when I attempted to shake the swarm into the box, for it was then that I had to have both arms free. Fortunately, the bees were not far from the main trunk of the oak tree and I was able to steady myself by leaning against it. I glanced quickly down to the ground and saw Cees edge his way out of the dropping zone. 'One, two, three now!' I said and gave the branch a lusty heave. The sudden and unexpected shock of ten pounds weight of bees landing in the box very nearly threw me off balance. Part of the swarm was safely trapped, and I rapidly fitted the lid, but there were still a lot of bees now buzzing angrily all round me. To my relief, and Cees's consternation, I saw that the loose bees were following the box as I lowered it to the ground. After I had succeeded in climbing down safely, we propped open one corner of the lid and watched them climb in happily to join the inmates. We knew then that we had the queen and that all was well.

That evening, having carefully prepared the new hive with suitable accommodation and a supply of sugar syrup, I carried the swarm up to the orchard. The next stage was to erect a flat board up which we hoped they would walk to the narrow slit, about nine inches from the ground, which formed the entrance to the hive. I knew that bees had a preference for white — hence the colour of beekeepers' outfits — so I covered the board with a sheet of white paper. Gently removing the top of the box, I held it upside down and gave it a sharp tap with my right hand. Most of the swarm landed as planned on the platform and a bit more shaking and tapping soon dislodged the rest of them. To my surprise, they accepted this rough treatment quite happily and there was no angry buzzing, such as invariably announces the presence of dive-bombing bees that are determined to commit *hari-kiri* on some particularly sensitive part of one's body. For a brief moment there was confusion; some bees ventured down the board, some went off to the right and others to the left. Then a few of the leading scouts reconnoitred up the board and quickly passed the message back that ahead of them lay the Promised Land. All heads were soon turned in that direction and the workers, drones and queen, who I glimpsed briefly in the centre of the leading wave, advanced in their thousands up the platform before disappearing from view.

By taking further swarms each year the population of bees and resulting jars of honey increased rapidly. Living on my own and being a rotten cook had its problems, but each day Cees and Hedy kindly allowed me to have lunch with them. Apart from this, eggs and honey washed down with a variety of alcoholic beverages formed the basis of my diet. Very little work with the bees was required, except during spring and early summer and, since I had no agricultural crops and allowed no spraying, there was an abundance of natural food for them. The main honey flow came in July, when the avenue of lime trees that grew alongside the road was alive with the buzzing of intoxicated bees.

Cees had always assisted with the various beekeeping jobs that were necessary, until one day he met his Waterloo in singularly painful circumstances. We were carrying out the first full inspection of the stocks on a sunny day in April and all had gone well with five of the six hives that we then had. Each one was queen-right and had a healthy brood with ample stocks of food. Furthermore, our protective clothing had so far succeeded in keeping several angry bees at bay. The sixth and final colony strongly resented our intrusion, and, despite massive puffs from the smoker, we were soon surrounded by vast numbers of extremely aggressive insects. Two bees got inside Cees's veil and stung him viciously on his nose and ear, while several poisoned darts penetrated through my gloves and into my wrists. Glancing at Cees's clothing to see whether there were any obvious chinks in his armour, I saw to my horror that half of his fly-buttons were undone. 'Cees!' I shouted. At that moment there was an almighty scream of *Godverdommen*, and he leapt into the air, clutching himself, and fled in disarray from the battlefield.

I have it on record from his wife that the damage was severe. And

A six-foot-eight Flying Dutchman.

from that day onwards his enthusiasm for beekeeping rapidly and understandably waned. After a couple of unsuccessful attempts to regain his confidence, he admitted to his terror of being stung again and firmly hung up his beekeeping outfit for the last time. Even then he was not safe from attack, for the bees clearly recognized in some remarkable way his phobia for them, and on several occasions, often quite far from the hives, he had to beat an undignified retreat. One would have thought that the smell of a petrol-driven lawn-mower would far outweigh that exuded by the jibbering giant who was operating the machine. The bees, however, invariably knew whether Cees or I were behind the machine and reacted accordingly. Maybe the 'nurse' bees passed on to succeeding generations of young workers the saga of the six foot eight flying Dutchman.

Cees and his family, despite the bees, settled happily into their rural existence at Daw's Hall. Not for them the bright lights, pubs and bingo halls. Cees's energy and stamina were amazing and, after a full day's work on the farm, he would continue to work outside until it was almost dark, tending his pygmy goats, chickens and Dutch call ducks, or doing a variety of jobs in his own garden. When the weather was foul, his spare time would be spent redecorating and improving the cottage, or poring over numerous bulb catalogues. Every so often Charlie, the postman, would bring little parcels to the door containing choice varieties of seeds, bulbs and plants, and Cees would tuck these lovingly into the folds of his enormous jersey before carrying them off to the seclusion of Rosabella Cottage. Even the most miserable little specimens responded to his green fingers and I found it demoralising to observe the obvious disparity in growth between identical plants grown by the two of us.

Gardeners, who are content to stuff a few bulbs into the soil and leave the rest to nature, can have no conception of the potential harvest ungarnered and the horticultural opportunities squandered. Cees would tie muslin nets over the heads of rare tulips and fritillaries to ensure protection for their seeds, and the resulting seedlings, carefully lifted, cleaned and replanted every autumn, would grow in time to mature, flower-bearing bulbs. Under his patient and loving care, these seeds were 'as the dust of the earth and. . . spread abroad to the west, and to the east, and to the north, and to the south,' or, less poetically, this meant the invasion, first of the kitchen garden, then a neighbouring plot of land and finally, when all existing resources had been used up, the purchasing by Cees and Hedy of four acres of unspoilt jungle just across the road from Daw's Hall. Lamarsh during spring began to resemble the bulb fields of Keukenhof.

In spite of my bad example, Cees's language remained remarkably unpolluted and English blasphemies hardly ever crossed his lips. He was of an exceptionally phlegmatic disposition and consequently on the rare occasions that I heard a scream of

Godverdommen, I knew that something really catastrophic had happened. One evening I was admiring the wonderful display of bulbs in his garden at Rosabella and he was proudly pointing out some of his latest acquisitions that were flowering for the first time, when the conversational tone of his voice abruptly changed and, biting hard on his cigar, the terrible oath rumbled forth.

'What's wrong?' I asked.

'Ach, *Godverdommen*,' he thundered once more. 'He's taken another of my *fritillaria pontica* buds and now I only haf two left.'

The notion of some kleptomaniac in our tiny hamlet who specialized in purloining the buds of rare bulbs seemed altogether too far-fetched. I inquired who he thought was responsible for the perpetration of this dastardly offence.

'Blue Boy,' he replied without hesitation, 'I haf to chase him off my garden every evening, and last veek I actually saw him eating the leaves of my rare five-leaf clover. I theenk we must shut him up in one of the empty pheasant aviaries.'

Well knowing who 'we' was, I dutifully went off in search of my fritillary-pilfering peacock. After a while I succeeded in locating him in the chicken house, where he was displaying to an admiring audience of Silkie hens, and duly caught him up and consigned him to the detention centre as instructed.

The following day, when I went down to lunch at the cottage, Cees appeared to have aged overnight and hardly uttered a word. Hedy broke the grim tidings to me: the pilferer had come again during the night and now only one flower-bud of *fritillaria pontica* remained. Ashen-faced, Cees announced that he wanted to borrow my shotgun and that he would maintain an armed vigil at the bathroom window every night, starting an hour before dawn and continuing until the intruder had been summarily despatched with a load of six-shot between the eyes. 'I theenk,' he said, 'it is one of the wild pheasants from the fields.'

Almost a whole week went by. The tiny petals of the fritillary began to unfurl, but still the thief had not revealed himself. Dark bags began to form beneath the eyes of its intrepid defender. I almost volunteered to relieve him, but decided that the responsibility was too great to shoulder.

Sadly, I didn't witness the climax to the saga and it was Hedy who later recounted the details to me. At six o'clock on a Sunday morning Cees had rushed into their bedroom and woken her with

Cees maintained an armed vigil at the bathroom window.

the triumphant news that he had killed the marauding
kleptomaniac.

'I never heard a shot,' she mumbled sleepily from the depths of
the bedclothes.

'I didn't use ze gun,' he replied and proceeded with his size
sixteen gumboots to reenact on the bedroom carpet how he had
stamped his adversary to death.

'What was it?' she asked.

'A slug.'

Cees's giant frame and outsize feet caused him a great problem when it came to clothing. Hedy, with considerable skill, managed to keep him provided with all his normal requirements, including a magnificent mauve evening shirt 'weeth frilse' and matching bow-tie, but the replacing of his boots for a long time defied even her ingenuity. The summer months were seldom a problem, for then Cees would wear huge, hand-made slippers, but winter and wet weather were times for more substantial footwear. First the toes and then the heels of his size eighteen, hand-knitted woollen socks began to peep through the extremities of his gumboots, and from that moment onwards there was a clear understanding who 'we' was when it came to aquatic work on the farm. I was soon as anxious as he was to secure replacements, but it was Hedy who eventually provided the solution. After requests to every accredited manufacturer of gumboots in the country had failed, she resorted to more subtle strategy and enlisted the support of the Press. The local newspaper carried a photograph of Cees, sitting on the grass outside Rosabella Cottage with his gargantuan feet almost protruding through the camera lens, and a heart-rending caption appealing for help in waterproof clothing for them. National papers and television picked up the story and in no time at all the Stapels were inundated with offers of assistance from leading gumboot makers in the country to widows of recently expired gentlemen of similar dimensions.

I now had the opportunity of buying a little more land, consisting of a few acres of dubious agricultural value across the river from the house. With this new acquisition I owned about sixty acres, equally divided between the counties of Suffolk and Essex. There was a footbridge across the Stour at the end of Pitmire Lane, so to walk round the farm was a brief and pleasant experience, but the conveying of heavy goods or machinery entailed a fifteen mile round trip by road.

This new land, apart from providing planting space for more poplars and cricket-bat willows, had a variety of other assets. I now owned over a mile of river bank and let the coarse fishing to the London Anglers' Association, whose members arrived by coach every weekend during the fishing season. The Association not only stocked the river but also provided a bailiff to keep the place tidy and see that the members behaved. By resisting attempts from the river authorities to dredge my stretch of the Stour and by putting neither pesticides nor artificial fertilizers on the land, the correct ecological balance was, I believe, preserved and an astounding wealth of wildlife took refuge in this oasis. The abundance of aquatic plants and small creatures provided ample food and shelter for the fish in the river, while the nettles, thistles and reeds growing along the banks harboured numerous insects and birds. In the summer holidays, Angus and Katrina had frequent picnics with me on the river banks and our enthusiastic forays with fishing rods and butterfly nets did little to reduce the population on the farm. Barn owls were a common sight over the water meadows, kingfishers and sand martins nested in the banks of the Stour, and occasionally we saw the spraint of an otter and on two occasions I had a fleeting glimpse of these enchanting and much persecuted animals. Badgers sometimes visited the farm, but so far we have not been lucky enough to have a set on our land. I hope that one day a pair will take up residence with us.

I gave up shooting game soon after moving to Daw's Hall as I found that I simply did not get the same enjoyment from it as I had when I was younger and more bloodthirsty, but both Cees and I had to wage a constant campaign against vermin. Jays and magpies, foxes and weasels, crows and rats can do irreparable damage on a wildfowl farm. I found that my early training under the gamekeeper at my old home in East Suffolk was invaluable, and devious tactics, many of which were not strictly legal, were employed against these predators. I salved my conscience somewhat by only waging war against them in the close vicinity of our birds. The local hunt were encouraged to have a bit of sport on my land, but they did little to reduce the number of foxes, many of which lived and bred in inaccessible thickets along the embankment of the railway line. My nine foot high perimeter fence provided good protection against them, but foxes that left unmistakable tracks along the outside of the wire were clearly up to no good and therefore better eliminated. Strong snares tied to the fencing posts accounted for one or two every year. One day the twelve year old son of some great friends in the village telephoned and asked whether he could come and shoot a few moorhens and rabbits on the farm, to which I readily agreed. As I was doing nothing particular that afternoon, I shouldered my game-bag and gun and set off with him to a marshy area on the farm which abounded with moorhens. We had only walked through this field for about twenty yards when up jumped a fox, almost from under

Barn owls were a common sight over the water meadows.

my feet, and he fell in his tracks to my gun only a few yards further on. I was going to leave it where it lay, but Nicky asked whether he could take the corpse home.

'What on earth are you going to do with it,' I asked. 'Put it in your parents' bed?'

After he had shot a couple of moorhens and missed a hare, Nicky set off for home with his trophy strapped to his bicycle. I would be seeing him later as I was dining with his parents that evening.

That they gave me a drink, let alone opened the door was remarkable. The fox had remained propped up on the pillows for well over an hour before Nicky's mother had gone up to change. By then the blood was seeping into the mattress. . .

Under Cees's sound management, our breeding successes on the farm gradually improved every year and there were few varieties of birds with which we had no luck whatever. Sales of young waterfowl and pheasants every autumn enabled us to buy new breeds and each winter more aviaries and ponds would be constructed and more planting carried out. It was not long before our price list showed over a hundred different varieties. Our population of ornamental pheasants increased particularly rapidly, though we found that in general they posed far greater problems than the waterfowl. Some of the cock birds could be murderously aggressive to us as well as their wives, and they were also much more susceptible to disease than the waterfowl. Some of these infections were certainly endemic to the soil, but others were carried by the wind or in the droppings of sparrows, starlings and other avian scavengers.

With the advice and encouragement of our vet, we decided to cover the ground in most of the pheasant aviaries with six inches of sand and to carry out a regular programme of preventive treatment against certain diseases. A mechanical dumper, hired from the local builder, was used for transporting the sand to each new block of aviaries before they were divided into individual pens, but there was no alternative to a wheelbarrow for the existing aviaries. Cees calculated that he personally shifted one hundred and fifty tons of sand in this fashion, a feat which must surely qualify for the *Guinness Book of Records*.

Once the work was completed, mud and disease were virtually eliminated and it was a simple enough operation to fork or rake the sand whenever the ground looked stale. Most important of all, this

Nicky rode off home with his trophy.

novel technique precluded the birds from ingesting any food or liquid except that which we prescribed for them. Thus, if we wanted to give all the pheasants their periodic treatment against fowl pest or parasitic worms, there would be no liquid available to them, in the form of grass or dew, except in their water bowls containing the drug.

By maintaining our pheasants in an almost sterile environment, their feed had of course to be carefully calculated and controlled. The basic diet for all of them was a pelleted turkey ration and corn or maize, administered every morning and afternoon, but they were also given during the breeding season an extra meal at lunch time, and this varied according to the day of the week, the time of year and the breed of bird. Some genera of pheasants in the wild state are insectivorous, some herbivorous and others omnivorous. Moreover, most animals and birds require a higher level of protein in their diet in the spring than they do at other times of the year. Mealworms, hard-boiled egg, fruit, green vegetables, onions and carrots were among the assorted rations kept in the foodshed.

The waterfowl were far easier to manage. After the departure of Henry, the cereopsis gander, to Whipsnade Zoo, the only aggressive breeds that we kept were black swans, a variety of shelduck and cape teal. Many varieties of geese can be temperamental, but limited grazing at the farm restricted our numbers. The black swans, which originate from Australia, were provided with a large pen and natural pond on the lawn in front of the house, and the other aggressive birds occupied smaller pens along the two streams leading into the main pond. Shelduck in the wild often nest down disused rabbit holes. We could provide neither rabbits nor rabbit holes where they were kept, so Cees constructed ingenious artificial tunnels with a trap-door at the end of each one, whereby we could collect the eggs. The waterfowl had breakfast and tea consisting of a basic diet comparable to that of the pheasants, but for lunch they had to forage for themselves. There was grass in all the enclosures, and frogspawn, acorns and aquatic insects were among the seasonal natural delicacies that they were able to find for themselves.

Only two ducks were given special rations and these were Mr and Mrs Eider. Believing that fish were essential for their well-being and capacity to breed on a muddy pond in East Anglia, I went off to a fishing village on the coast every year in November with a friend who kept both eiders and mergansers. There we would buy half a ton of sprats from the fishermen and on our return home, would put them into small polythene bags and stock them in my friend's enormous, walk-in deep freeze.

Every day for three years Mr and Mrs Eider were given their daily quota of sprats and, although it was a joy to watch their remarkable underwater gymnastics at feed time, they never made the slightest attempt to nest. The fourth year the fishermen had a very poor sprat harvest, the price of the fish trebled and we reluctantly decided that our eiders and mergansers would have to make do on rather more plebeian rations. That spring Mrs Eider disappeared and a search revealed her to be sitting on a pile of eiderdown and four large, olive-green eggs. When these were removed and placed under one of my larger matrons from the hen-house, she laid two further clutches and every single egg hatched. Cees and I agreed that she and her husband must, in the past, have been far too concerned about missing out on their daily sprats to turn their minds to the basic subject of sex.

Chapter Six

To climb the trackless mountains all unseen,
With the wild flock that never needs a fold,
Alone o'er steeps and foaming falls to lean,
This is not solitude; 'tis but to hold
Converse with Nature's charms, and view her stores unrolled.

Byron

There are times when all of us are seized with a sudden and overwhelming desire to escape. Some take to the sea, others to drink; but when it happens to me, I like to climb to some remote place, where I can breathe deeply the cool, mountain air and bask in the knowledge that the vast majority of the human race are several thousand feet below me.

As a boy I spent many enchanted hours walking over the fells in the Lake District and tramping across MacGillycuddy's Reeks in Ireland. I am very ignorant of the true art of mountaineering and prone to an instant attack of vertigo at the mere mention of a *couloir* or *bergschrund*, but even so, the sight of a mountain range has always sent a tingling, challenging sensation through my spine.

During my first tour with the King's African Rifles, most of our time had been spent operating against Mau Mau gangs in the Aberdare Forest in Kenya, and one of the most soothing and spectacular sights in that area was the snow clad peaks of Mount Kenya. During the day its summit was usually shrouded in mist and cloud, but most evenings there was a glorious moment when the drapery briefly parted. The mountain then stood exposed in all its glory, before descending darkness drew the curtain back across the stage. Two hundred miles further south, in what was then

94

Tanganyika, stood Kilimanjaro, whose crest, resembling a huge Christmas pudding with brandy butter dripping down the sides, rose to close on twenty thousand foot. In 1954, during one of our rare periods of leave during the Emergency, four brother officers and I planned to try and climb to the summit. Although all of us were extremely fit after months of jungle bashing in the Aberdares, we nevertheless contrived to arrive at the starting-gate in rather less than tiptop condition. Forty-eight hours of intense and delightful dissipation in the flesh-pots of Nairobi, while *en route* to the foothills, had considerably sapped our energy. While we were checking our equipment and bathing our aching eyeballs in the rest-house at Arusha, a veritable termagant of a woman accosted us. Without so much as asking whether we minded, she announced that as she could find no other climbing companions she intended to accompany us up the mountain the following day. I once saw a photograph in some paper of the female commandant of one of Hitler's concentration camps for Jews and the face and physique bore a close resemblance to that of our new mountaineering companion. She was ruggedly blond, hirsute and Teutonic, and earned her living teaching gymnastics at the local European girls' school. Having been at the rest house for two days and having learned from the proprietor of our impending arrival, she had already made contact with our guides and porters and arranged that we should start the ascent at seven the following morning. All we had to do, apparently, was to get out of our beds and follow Olga up the mountain like good little boys, humming the strains of *Deutschland, Deutschland.*

The first two days went by quite happily. After climbing gradually up through the forest, where hornbills, turacos and inquisitive monkeys watched us from the trees, we eventually came to open moorland and saw for the first time the twin peaks of Kibo and Mawenzi. The mountain air was exhilarating, the scenery marvellous and morale high. Tired out after each day's strenuous exertions, we camped in well constructed cabins along the trail, where even the sight of Olga doing press-ups and deep-breathing exercises while we collapsed onto our sleeping bags and slaked our thirst on innumerable cans of beer, did little to destroy the general harmony. On the third day, the ascent was much steeper, the atmosphere became noticeably more rarified and tempers began to get somewhat frayed. We arrived, blistered and exhausted, at Camp

3, just below the snow-line, with all but one member of the party feeling the extremely unpleasant symptoms of mountain sickness. The exception of course was Olga, and all of us would, if we had had the strength, have willingly throttled her with our bare hands rather than have to endure the sight of her doing limbering-up exercises for the summit. We started the final assault an hour before dawn with Olga and the two African guides striding resolutely forward in the lead and the rest of us, with aching limbs and splitting headaches, stumbling along in the rear. Suddenly, there was a cry of anguish from the front and the next thing we saw was Olga being given a fireman's lift by one of the guides back to Camp 3. Her sacrifice, however, was not in vain. Spurred on by her downfall, the three of us who were least affected by mountain sickness, struggled onwards and upwards to the highest point on the continent.

Fifteen years later, the yearning and the opportunity came to me simultaneously for a comparable mountain trek. By 1970 Daw's Hall Wildfowl Farm had a fairly comprehensive collection of waterfowl and pheasants, the latter in particular including nearly all the ornamental breeds available. There were, as I well knew, a number of exciting varieties lurking in virtually inaccessible regions, such as Vietnam and the Chinese Peoples' Republic, and it was to these that my ever fertile imagination began to turn. One genus in particular, the blood pheasants, of which thirteen different races were known to science, had, despite several previous attempts, never been successfully kept or bred in captivity anywhere in the world. The London Zoo had received a pair in 1875, one of which remained alive for just over a year, and this constituted the record until almost a century later, when an English breeder whom I knew had kept a hen bird alive for seventeen months, the cock bird having expired shortly after arrival. Jean Delacour, probably the foremost authority on pheasants in the world, had written that it was 'extremely doubtful whether these beautiful birds will ever be kept and reared successfully far from their native haunts.'

The native haunts of the blood pheasant in fact cover a vast and forbidding area — the mountain ranges of the Himalayas, eastwards and northwards into Tibet and Communist China. Armed with my old army sleeping-bag, a strong pair of boots and three mist-nets, I flew off to Kathmandu, in the early spring of

1970. The blood pheasants at that time of the year live at altitudes of around eleven or twelve thousand feet and are nowhere common. Finding a covey, let alone trapping live birds was no simple operation in an area where only yaks and Sherpas move with any degree of ease. To complicate matters further, an unexpectedly heavy fall of snow rendered almost any form of movement impossible for a week. During this time my guide and I were marooned, first in a cave and then in a native hut, while the snow lay waist-deep all around us. We were sustained by a few handfuls of rice and potatoes, a single bar of chocolate and several bottles of highly potent *raxshi*. More intoxicating than any drink were the silence and the scenery. No wireless, no telephone, no traffic — instead the majestic snow-clad mountains and the music of ice blue waters cascading over great boulders on the long journey down to the sea. Clearly visible to the north was the summit of Everest itself.

When the thaw finally came, great blocks of snow fell from the trees and cliff-tops crashing down into the valleys below, the birds began to sing and our search for the blood pheasants continued. The full account of two uncomfortable but exhilarating months that I spent in one of the most beautiful and unspoilt regions on earth has already been described in my previous book*. It closes with a pair of optimistically named birds, Hima and Laya, poised for their flight back to England. The birds reached Daw's Hall alive, but both sadly perished within a short while of their arrival.

From Kathmandu, I had flown on to Darjeeling. There, I had come across an Indian trapper, who had confidently announced that the collection of blood pheasants was a perfectly simple operation and that he would write to me in England when he next had some for sale.

About nine months after my return home a somewhat cryptic telegram was delivered to Daw's Hall: 'HAVE MANY MANY BLOOD PHEASANTS. PLEASE COME TOMORROW. SHRESTHA' The telegram, I noticed, had been despatched thirty six hours previously. Frantically, I searched the house for the scrumpled piece of paper on which I knew I had written his address. Having turned the place upside down and emptied every drawer in the study, I eventually found it at the bottom of my

Blood Pheasant 1971

rucksack. Not only did it contain his address in Darjeeling but also, to my surprise, his telephone number. While munching my usual high tea of four beautiful fresh-laid eggs, toast and honey from my bees, I was feverishly racking my brains and trying to work out the best plan of action. Impetuosity may well be a vice, but I have always considered it a lesser and far more exciting evil than dithering. Brushing the crumbs from my face, I grabbed the telephone.

'Operator, get me a call to Darjeeling 318, please; and it's urgent.'

There was a pause at the other end of the line, and then the lady from the GPO said 'There aren't any three figure Darlington numbers, sir.'

'No, I want Darjeeling, which is in India,' I explained, trying hard not to be too patronising.

'Hold on, sir, I'll connect you to International.'

While waiting for what seemed an eternity, I had awful visions of Mr and Mrs Pradeep Shrestha and lots of little baby Shresthas eating my precious blood pheasants for their dinner since I had not met the deadline. Eventually a new voice came on the line and I repeated the number that I wanted.

'Call you back,' he replied in an infuriatingly composed and matter-of-fact tone of voice. The line went dead and there was nothing for it but to pour myself another cup of tea and wait. Twice the telephone rang, but one was a wrong number and the other was my bank manager, suggesting that I might like to call in and have a little chat with him about my overdraft when I was next in Sudbury. I tried to keep calm by reading the newspaper, but could not concentrate. I did, however, notice a small paragraph on 'Crippling strikes and acute political unrest in many parts of India.'

At last the call came through. I was connected to a telephone operator in Calcutta who announced that he was ringing the number in Darjeeling for me. Calcutta was coming through loud and clear, but communications over the final five hundred miles of telephone line through to the strike-ridden province of West Bengal appeared to be posing problems. I could hear Calcutta and so, I gathered, could Shrestha, but any intelligible form of conversation between the two of us was impossible. Occasional snippets came through and I distinctly heard him say 'seventeen birds' and 'how many rupees you pay?'

When Shrestha and the operator were not screaming at each other in some high-pitched foreign tongue, I succeeded in getting the latter to relay up to Darjeeling that he must keep all the birds for me and that I was leaving immediately. As I put the receiver back on the hook my hand was shaking horribly. I only then noticed that Cees had walked into the kitchen.

'Vere are you going now?' he asked in an amused tone of voice. He had for a long time been the ideal foil to some of my wilder eccentricities.

I took a gulp of tepid tea and replied, in a voice weak from nervous exhaustion, 'India.' And then, spelling it out slowly, 'seventeen blood pheasants are sitting in Darjeeling for us.'

'Seventeen? *Godverdommen*!'

Excitement on the farm was intense as we quickly made plans for my departure from London Airport the following evening. It was my intention to be away for as short a time as possible and I told Cees that I hoped to be home within a week, or ten days at the outside. There was only one problem that I could see and that was how I was going to pay, not only for a flight for myself half way round the world, but for the birds and freight charges for them back to England. After some quick mental arithmetic, I worked out that I should have little change out of fifteen hundred pounds. I discussed this, as I did all my other many problems, with Cees and Hedy over a drink that evening and they very sensibly suggested that I try to form a syndicate of backers. There was no time to waste, so I rang up several friends that night and put the proposition to them. Why any of them should have agreed to squander their money on such a hare-brained scheme, I have never been able to understand, but within half an hour I was guaranteed, in varying shares, three-quarters of all the expenses that would be incurred. The agreement was that any birds that I succeeded in getting home would be the joint property of all of us. The only hope of any dividends for shareholders lay in the extremely unlikely eventuality of our breeding and selling offspring. The remaining quarter share I had decided to keep for myself, but when Cees was driving me to the station the following afternoon, he said that Hedy and he would very much like to take a small investment in the gamble. I happily made over a share to them and boarded the train to London.

Thirty six hours later I was travelling in another train, this time on the narrow gauge 'Toy' Railway which, with a delightful combination of charm and chuff, struggles upwards from the sweltering, tropical plains into the foothills of the Himalayas. Constructed between 1879 and 1881 as a more salubrious means of travel than by bullock-cart to 'the Queen of the Hill Stations', this railway line is one of the most remarkable in the world. So steep are some of the gradients that the train has to go through the most extraordinary contortions, sometimes literally chasing its own tail, as it winds its way laboriously upwards to Ghoom, at 7,407 foot, before the final downhill run into Darjeeling. There, a faded placard advertising the Upper Class Ladies Waiting Room struck a somewhat archaic and incongruous note.

As soon as I had booked into a hotel, I asked the sari-clad receptionist to be kind enough to get me a call to Darjeeling 318.

'I am very, very sorry, sir, but the telephone exchange is on strike. Maybe start work again next week,' she added, as though to remind me that in India all things are possible, given time, money and plenty of patience.

Thankful that I had managed to contact Shrestha from England before the telephone operators had downed head-sets, I set off on foot down the street towards the centre of the town where he lived. Strenuously avoiding the solicitations of the usual throng of beggars and curio sellers along the route, I made my way safely to his house and knocked on the door. There was no reply. I tried again, louder this time, and heard childrens' voices from within. There was a pause and then the door opened and I found myself being inspected by a wide-eyed and rather frightened boy of about seven years of age.

'Mr. Pradeep Shrestha?' I enquired.

'Yes, he is my father.'

'Is he at home?' I asked.

I saw the boy look hesitantly over his shoulder and then he said 'He is sleeping. Maybe you come back tomorrow.'

At that moment I heard the tinkling of broken glass and the sound of a muffled oath from within. Holding a bottle of whisky in one hand, the tall figure of Pradeep Shrestha weaved his way unsteadily towards the door.

'Ah, Major Grahm, welcome sho' Zharzheeling.' The words were interspersed with the occasional hiccup, and an overpowering smell of alcohol and beetle-nut wafted towards me. 'Come in and have a zhrink. Whisky, vodka, beer. . .?'

I settled for a bottle of beer, which Shrestha managed with some difficulty to open and pour into a glass while yelling at his son to tidy up the debris and fetch another chair. Impatient to know the score regarding the birds and aware that time was precious if I was to receive a reasonably coherent and accurate report, I came straight to the point. He said that there were indeed seventeen blood pheasants which his men had trapped over the border in Nepal and that they were at present with his brother, who lived two days walk up into the hills. His innate oriental trader's instinct was obviously immune to the effects of alcohol. A ridiculous price was named, but this customary opening bid was, I knew, merely part of the time-honoured convention and likely to bear little relationship to the final contract. After several drinks and a good deal of haggling, an agreed price was reached and I insisted, not only that he made the necessary arrangement for the birds to stay in the Darjeeling Zoo until they were fit for the long journey home, but also that the actual payment for them be deferred until they were safely on board an aeroplane. As events turned out, it was fortunate that I made these stipulations.

Early the following morning I set off with a guide for the village where the blood pheasants were being held. My rucksack contained my sleeping bag, sheets of foam rubber for protecting the birds heads on the walk back to Darjeeling, a thick jersey, spare pair of socks, first aid equipment (both human and avian), water flask, three packets of biscuits and loads of glucose tablets. Shrestha had given me a letter to take to his brother, instructing him to arrange porters and carrying baskets for the pheasants. Although he assured me that the journey could not be done in less than two days each way, I told him it was essential, if the birds were to reach Darjeeling in good condition and I was to pay him all those rupees, that the descent be done in one day.

The first part of our journey was by jeep. After a brief climb up the mountainside in bottom gear we came to a crest and before us, sprawling like a gigantic snake, the road twisted and meandered in a series of hairpin bends down to the valley far, far below. Alongside the track, trees festooned with moss and lichen provided an abundance of food for titmice, orioles and laughing thrushes, while high overhead a pair of white-backed vultures circled lazily in the clear blue sky. The driver had hardly impressed me on the upward climb and I feared that we might well be in for a hair-raising descent. I uttered a silent prayer that he would engage a low gear and steer a course that kept us as far as possible from the lips of successive, yawning precipices. My prayers were not answered. No sooner had we reached the summit than the driver slapped the gear-lever into neutral and switched off the ignition. The jeep silently moved off downhill and soon there was a horrible smell of burning rubber as we free-wheeled down the mountainside with the brakes as our only lifeline. After two or three nightmarish corners I could bear it no longer and told him, in no uncertain terms to switch on the ignition immediately and to drive in first or second gear. Much to my relief he obliged, but then came the rider: 'Sahib, petrol cost very many rupees. If engine used for driving down hills, all taxi fares double.' My retort is unprintable.

At last we reached the point where the road ended and a footpath took over. Gangs of coolies, sweating in the hot sun with pickaxe and shovel, were in the process of hacking a further extension for motor vehicles out of the hillside, but a recent landslide of huge boulders had, fortunately for me, held up their progress. It was but a short walk to the village where one of Shrestha's many brothers resided and where I hoped our next form of transport would be waiting for us.

For the first time since leaving Darjeeling I was able to relax and enjoy the marvellous scenery. Away to the north, as if suspended between earth and sky lay the massive peaks of Kanchenjunga, whose summit is only a thousand foot lower than that of Everest. Much of the ground below it was encased in a thick blanket of cloud, but beneath the cloud vast forests of pine and birch, juniper and rhododendron, covered the steep hillsides. Clearly visible through my fieldglasses were myriads of waterfalls that tumbled and cascaded down the mountainsides, carrying the melted snow from the Himalayas down to the mighty Ganges and Bramaputra and on to the Bay of Bengal. It was hard to appreciate that the murky, turgid waters, that I had seen two days previously flowing through the streaming tropical plains around Calcutta, had their origins in these ethereal rooftops of the world.

Shrestha'a brother was eventually located and was both charming and, to my relief, sober. There was, he explained, a small problem: the two best ponies were lame and it would take fifteen minutes for his son to go and collect replacements from a friend's house. A small figure disappeared into the distance with a couple of halters, while another appeared with bottles of the ubiquitous Pepsi Cola. Three hours and several Pepsi Colas later the small boy eventually returned, dragging behind him two ancient and emaciated animals. The guide and I mounted and set off into the hills followed by a large crowd of children urging the poor beasts to keep up a reasonable pace. It was soon apparent that this was beyond them, so we sent the ponies back to the village and continued on foot. In spite of the delays we succeeded in arriving at our destination late in the afternoon of the second day. The little village was perched on top of a steep hill, at a height of about nine thousand feet, and away in the distance, temporarily freed from the shackles of mist and cloud, lay the whole chain of the snow-covered Himalayas, home of the little partridge-sized birds that I had travelled four thousand miles to collect.

It is a sad reflection on civilized man that the more primitive an ethnic society and the more remote its habitat, the more attractive generally is the nature of its members. I had seen this many times with African tribes and more recently on my expedition into Nepal. The unfettered ways of the inhabitants of the tiny hillside hamlet where I was to spend the night were a marked contrast to those of their countrymen that I had seen at lower altitudes. This simple agricultural community struggled hard and selflessly to earn a living by tilling the soil on the steep terraced hillside, deriving strength and inspiration from their fervent belief in the bonds of family, religion and time-honoured customs.

The blood pheasants were all grouped together in a converted chicken house with slatted bamboo sides and corrugated iron roofing. They looked healthy and contented and it was a wonderful sight to see them feeding happily on freshly cut bamboo leaves, rice grains and grass. There were a few shrill calls of alarm as I cautiously inspected them, but they soon settled down again to their evening feed. The hens, of which there were nine, had the soft brown colouring of fallen leaves in autumn, while the cock birds were a subtle mixture of dove-grey and palest yellow merging to green. The throats, the legs and the areas round the eyes of the eight males were vivid red, and flecks of the same blood colouring adorned their breasts.

'You pleased with pheasants?' enquired Shrestha's brother,

Himalayan blood pheasants.

Prem. 'My trappers collect them two weeks ago up there across the border in Nepal,' and he pointed to an area where the long evening shadows on the distant hills merged with the pink and purple snow-line of the Himalayas.

It was difficult to express my feelings in words. I was all too conscious that at that moment I had both the luck and privilege to be looking at something unique, a captive collection of seventeen specimens of a bird which, to the best of my knowledge, was represented nowhere else in the world outside their natural habitat. My thoughts raced back to my previous expedition; to the excitement, the discomfort and the eventual feelings of failure and frustration when the two birds that I had eventually succeeded in getting to England had died within a short while of their arrival. I just hoped that their demise had not been in vain and that, through having observed them in the wild in Nepal, and having studied carefully their diet, their habits and their reaction to captivity, Cees and I could now succeed where generations of other aviculturists had failed.

'Yes,' I said quietly, 'I am very, very pleased.'

After a delicious supper of curried goat and a comfortable night curled up in my sleeping bag by the dying embers of the fire, we set off an hour after dawn the next morning. I had arranged with the jeep driver to meet us at the end of the track at four o'clock that afternoon and I knew that by making a forced march we could get there on time. The previous evening Prem's wife had sewn the foam rubber padding into the bamboo baskets, so it was a simple matter to catch the birds and load them onto the backs of four porters. We made good time on the downward journey and, since I had insisted on deferring Jehu's payment until we had safely returned to Darjeeling, he was waiting at the rendezvous as planned.

As soon as we reached Darjeeling I collected Pradeep Shrestha from his house and drove with him and my precious cargo to the zoo. Shrestha had arranged for a pair of vultures to be moved to a different enclosure and it was into their covered aviary that I planned to deposit my blood pheasants.

The zoo was indescribably dirty and badly managed and it took until just before dark that evening to clean and disinfect the aviary. I was told that the zoo staff came on duty at seven-thirty each morning, so I arranged to meet the bird keepers there at that time the following day to supervise the feeding and watering of my birds. The zoo gates were open when I arrived — perhaps they were never closed — but it was past ten o'clock before the first member of the staff arrived. While waiting, I walked round all the pens and enclosures and watched as the arrival of the sun brought hordes of flies onto the decomposing remains of food and faeces in the various cages. A pair of emaciated Siberian tigers, of which there are probably less than two hundred surviving in the world, lay panting for water beside their empty drinking trough. Ill-treatment and senseless exploitation of any living creature is something that invariably makes me angry and by the end of my tour of inspection my blood was boiling. Having administered to the needs of the blood pheasants and having given them, in their water, certain drugs that I had brought from England to relieve the recent stress of handling and travel, I demanded to be taken to the superintendent of the zoo. A fat, unctious specimen of humanity, he had just got out of bed and was yawning sleepily in his pyjamas when I walked into the office which was part of his house. The ensuing diatribe that I delivered had at least some effect. The zoo staff were mobilised into unprecedented activity, scrubbing brushes and disinfectant were brought into use and, for the rest of my stay in Darjeeling, the keepers turned up punctually every morning. I insisted too that the vet be called in to treat birds and mammals that were obviously ailing. The latter was a charming man, who had qualified in England, but he lacked the authority and encouragement to do what he knew from his training to be necessary.

It was my plan to spend no more than three or four days in Darjeeling, since I calculated that this was sufficient time for the blood pheasants to become acclimatized to a lower altitude before the homeward journey to England. Accordingly, with the help of Shrestha, I arranged for the local *fundi* to build plywood boxes suitable for transportation of the birds and made the necessary booking for my own flight. Shrestha, himself, used every known oriental ruse to extract from me the price that we had agreed, but I insisted that he adhere to the bargain and take payment only when the birds were safely loaded onto an aeroplane. Four hours by road from Darjeeling lay a small airstrip at Bagdogra, from where there were flights twice daily to the international airport just outside Calcutta. Shrestha arranged for a taxi to take us on the first stage of the journey. The steaming heat of Calcutta would, I knew, be the most testing time for these creatures of the high Himalayas but, by catching the late afternoon flight from Bagdogra, we would be travelling at the coolest part of the day.

When the appointed day came for us to depart from Darjeeling there was great activity at the zoo. All the staff turned up an hour early and vied with one another to assist me in loading nutrition and birds into the boxes. Even the superintendent was present, with a sycophantic smile on his face, waiting like all the others for the customary *buckshees*. In the cramped quarters of the adjacent pen the pair of evicted vultures awaited our departure with equally avaricious expressions on their faces.

By mid-morning we were all packed up and ready to go. The journey to Bagdogra was downhill nearly all the way, but the word had clearly got round the taxi stalls of Darjeeling that I was one *Sahib* on whom the game of double-fare-for-use-of-engine was not to be recommended. We progressed at a comfortable pace, at first following and frequently crossing the 'Toy' railway line on which I had travelled up the previous week. Gradually the alpine vegetation of magnolias, rhododendrons and tree-ferns gave way to more tropical plants. Finally we came to an escarpment and down below us the road straightened and a heat haze hung over the arid plains for as far as the eye could see. When the town of Bagdogra eventually came into view, Shrestha's voluble conversation turned to the subject of the celebration party he was planning on his return to Darjeeling that evening.

As we approached the airstrip, the small aeroplane was clearly visible outside the corrugated tin shack that served as the arrival and departure lounge. I looked at my watch. Exactly one hour before the flight was due to leave. We drove up to the shack, unloaded the crates of blood pheasants and placed them beneath the shade of some tall palm trees. While the driver and I stood guard over them and endeavoured to shift the inevitable crowd of garrulous Indians who were trying to inspect the birds through the air-holes in their plywood boxes, Shrestha went off to check that the flight was leaving on time. As he walked back towards us, I could sense from the crestfallen expression on his face that we had a problem.

'*Sahib*,' he said lugubriously, 'very very big troubles. All Indian Airline pilots have gone on strike.'

'Since when?' I asked, hardly able to believe my ears.

'They stop all flights from midday today. This aeroplane here,' he explained, 'just left here by pilot after morning flight from Calcutta. Pilot go away home until strike is ended.'

'And when do they think the strike will end?' I asked.

'Maybe tomorrow. Airport manager try to ring Dum Dum Airport but telephone operators on strike again. I think best we stay night in Bagdogra hotel and come here again in morning.'

'Want a bet that the hotel staff are on strike too?' I enquired testily.

Shrestha's idea of staying the night in Bagdogra was one alternative, another was to take the taxi on to Calcutta. However, when the driver told me it would take twenty hours and stated the fare, for which I could have bought the taxi outright, I quickly abandoned this idea. Speed of travel and the shortest possible time in the crippling heat of the lowland plains were, I knew, vital to the well-being of the birds. For this reason, I decided against staying any longer in Bagdogra. Not only was there no guarantee that flights would be resumed in the morning, but feeding and watering the pheasants would be likely to pose an awful problem.

'Pradeep,' I said, 'There is only one thing to do.'

'You pay me now and stay night in very, very good Bagdogra hotel?' he enquired hopefully.

'No, I'm sorry, but I'm not going to do that. We are all going back to Darjeeling now.'

Slowly and in almost total silence we retraced our journey along the twisting, bumpy track that climbs about five thousand feet in a hundred miles. The streets of Darjeeling were deserted as we drove into the town just after midnight. I directed the driver to go straight to the zoo and told Shrestha to find the keeper who had the key to my aviary.

I should, of course have left the birds in their boxes till first light, but I just could not wait to know what toll the long drive and six hours in that stifling heat had taken of them. For about an hour there was pandemonium; feathers flew and it was impossible to say who made the most noise — the pyjama-clad zoo keepers, the petrified vultures or the monkeys in an adjoining pen — as I endeavoured to direct operations by the light of a flickering torch. Eventually the blood pheasants were safely back in their pen and Shrestha was clearly as relieved as I was that, by some incredible

108

stroke of good fortune, all the birds had survived their ordeal. When everyone else had gone off to bed, I lingered for a while, listening silently to the happy little calls of the pheasants hopping up onto their bamboo perches to sleep.

The next two weeks were monotonous and frustrating. Every morning and every afternoon I walked the half mile up to the zoo to feed my birds on diced apple, chopped hard-boiled egg, fresh grass and bamboo leaves. Each day, too, I walked in the opposite direction to the office of Indian Airlines in the town, where the answer to my enquiries was always 'maybe tomorrow'. There were the occasional moments of relief and one of them was the magnificent sight of Kanchenjunga at sunset, immediately followed by a series of outstandingly good martinis in the hotel.

On the tenth day, which was two days before Christmas, Indian Airlines announced that normal flights were to be resumed the next day. The telephone operators had just completed their strike, so I was able to send one telegram to Cees, telling him to expect me on Christmas Day, and another to the children wishing them a happy Christmas and saying that I hoped to see them very soon.

Up at the zoo, the staff eagerly awaited their second lot of *buckshees*, while Shrestha booked the taxi to take us to Bagdogra and arranged the new date for his celebration party. Tomorrow, however, took a further four days to come so far as services between Bagdogra and Calcutta were concerned. When the strike had started, the pilots had abandoned their aeroplanes wherever they happened to be at the time and had quietly taken French leave. Our particular pilot was, I understood, enjoying himself in Ceylon and was loath to cut short his holiday. This time I could not send any more telegrams to Cees as the telephone operators had once again done the inevitable. Christmas was a desultory celebration with tinned Indian turkey, tinned Chinese Christmas pudding and a very drunk Shrestha, whom I had been rash enough to invite to the hotel for dinner.

When the day finally came for our second departure, Shrestha announced that he would not be coming to Bagdogra as his sister was getting married. I therefore deposited the money that I owed him with his bank manager with written instructions that it should only be paid out after twenty four hours had elapsed. By then I knew that we should either be back in Darjeeling or safely airborne. I also left clear instructions at the zoo that no vultures,

A lammergeier, or bearded vulture, with Kanchenjunga in the background.

porcupines, tigers or any other creatures were to be moved into the blood pheasants' aviary until midday the following day. The parting valedictions showered on me by Shrestha and all the staff of Darjeeling Zoo were heartfelt and painfully sincere.

The taxi ride to the outskirts of Bagdogra was uneventful and, having already completed a trial run without any harm befalling the birds, I was much less concerned over their reaction to the first stage of the journey as I was to the five hours that we were due to spend in Calcutta.

At the outskirts of Bagdogra and about five miles from the airstrip I noticed an enormous throng of people ahead of us. As we drove closer to them, we could see that they had formed a solid human blockade against all traffic. We came to a halt thirty yards or so from the edge and I told the driver to go and find out what was going on. He returned, several shades paler and shaking with terror, to say that there was a forced strike of all public transport for twenty-four hours and that any vehicles that did not conform were to be set alight by the roadisde. Pointing a little way down the road, he indicated another angry mob gathered around the smouldering remains of a bus.

'I'm bloody well not going back to Darjeeling again,' I said, more in desperation than with any feeling of conviction. 'Get back into the taxi, drive up to them and tell them that I've got to get through or we shall miss the aeroplane.'

'No, no, no, *Sahib*,' the poor man wailed, 'I have many, many children and nobody else to care for them. Also, I am too much frightened,' he added, in case I hadn't noticed.

I chose this moment to lose my temper completely and, without thought for the consequences, I literally hurled the unfortunate driver into the back of his taxi, jumped into the driving seat and switched on the ignition. The crowd must have sensed my blind rage for there was a sudden silence as I put her into gear and hurtled forwards.

An obvious ringleader, waving a tattered green banner, stood right in the centre of the road and, with my foot hard on the accelerator, I drove straight at him. Pandemonium broke out as he and others struggled to leap out of my way. A couple of bricks came through the side window, showering us with broken glass and sending my reluctant passenger into a stage of gibbering hysteria. The blood pheasants in their boxes joined in the chorus, but

111

fortunately neither we nor they sustained a direct hit. The mob around the burned bus had even less time to react, for I was in top gear by then and accelerating fast. A mile further down the road was the welcome sight of a company of troops, bristling with arms and firmly dispersing another crowd of insurgents. Their commander detailed off one platoon to escort us to the airport and promised to see that the driver was given safe conduct back through the town after I had boarded the aeroplane.

Exactly twenty-three hours after leaving Darjeeling, seventeen specimens of *Ithagenis cruentus* and one of *Homo sapiens*, all equally exhausted, arrived safely at Daw's Hall.

Chapter Seven

After the blood pheasants had recovered from their long journey and had appeared to have adjusted to the change of altitude, weather conditions and diet, we moved them into their permanent quarters. While they are not, so far as is known, endangered in the wild, it was obviously important to carry out and record proper experiments on the behaviour of these strange creatures, of which little more than the occasional museum skin was currently known to science. Cees and I were equally conscious of our unique opportunity to add to this knowledge. Our ultimate aim was naturally to breed from these birds and establish a viable captive population, but we were under no illusions of the magnitude of the task that confronted us.

Among the many ideas we discussed, it seemed sensible, in view of the number of blood pheasants that we possessed, to test whether the strong covey instinct, which had been so apparent when I had seen them in the wild on my original visit to the Himalayas, persisted during the breeding season. No wild creature is likely to breed in captivity unless it is reasonably happy with its environment. By dispersing the birds initially to different types of aviaries, we hoped to further our knowledge as to the most suitable environment for them.

One hen died shortly after arrival from some mysterious liver complaint and that left us with eight pairs. Three pairs were isolated in three separate aviaries where their only communication with their friends was by voice. Three further pairs were placed in adjoining aviaries, where they could both hear and see their companions on either side. The remaining two pairs, which we banded with distinctive coloured rings on one leg, were given the run of three contiguous aviaries, each approximately forty square metres in size, in which a series of loopholes in the wire netting enabled the birds to pass freely between all three aviaries if they so wished. The males of almost all species of pheasant are extremely pugnacious to other cock pheasants, particularly during the breeding season, and the normal practice is to segregate each pair (or trio, if they are polygamous by nature). I was well aware that we could be courting disaster in the 'loophole' pens.

The days were now getting longer and warmer. The trees began to come into leaf, butterflies emerged from their long winter's sleep and the thrushes in the garden were busy lining their nests with dung and rotten wood. Cees and I busied ourselves checking, disinfecting and repairing where necessary all the hatching and rearing equipment that would soon be needed. By the second week in March the thrushes' nests contained their quota of four or five greenish-blue, blotched eggs and a fortnight later the early birds on the farm — Edwards' and Swinhoe's pheasants, the whistle-sneezing Carolinas and Mr and Mrs Barbarossa — started to lay their first clutches. Spring is the busiest and yet the most exciting time on the farm, and this year particularly it was a time of great expectations.

Early morning and late evening are the best moments to walk quietly round the aviaries and enclosures and watch the waterfowl and pheasants indulging in their displays of courtship and territorial aggression. Spring is also the noisiest time of the year, with Blue Boy invariably sounding the alarm call with a series of piercing, demoniacal screams sharp at five o'clock every morning. To me the most thrilling and nostalgic notes in the farm orchestra came from the aviaries that housed the blood pheasants. The isolated pairs made plenty of noise, but their calling seemed to us to have a plaintive tone, as though they were continually trying to re-establish contact with the rest of the covey. The pairs occupying adjacent 'semi-detacheds' spent much of their time pacing up and down the wire netting that divided them from their neighbours, while the happiest group was clearly the quartet of 'loopholers'.

Though most of our pheasants were by this time being kept on sand, all the blood pheasant aviaries were intentionally still down to grass. The two pairs in the loophole pens, while living and moving together in close harmony during January and February, began to establish separate territories in the two outside aviaries as

114

spring got under way, grazing these pens till the grass was like a lawn. The middle pen became a no man's land, and the grass there remained virtually untouched. Sometimes a cock, or cock plus hen, would sally forth into the adjoining aviaries and these incursions elicited much chasing activity and phrenetic sexual displays by the two males, directed sometimes to either of the two females and sometimes, rather surprisingly, to each other.

Apart from weekends, when I managed single-handed, and Wednesdays, when I endeavoured to bury my head under the pillow for an hour longer, it was normal practice for Cees and I to spend the start of each day together on the farm. All the animals and birds had to be fed and watered, the daily routine had to be planned and there was often some crisis to be resolved that had occurred since the previous evening. Perhaps a fox had tried to burrow under the perimeter fence during the night, or a stoat had got in and killed a duck, or a hen pheasant had received over-amorous attention from her husband and required stitches in her scalp, or a host of other eventualities. Sometimes, too, there would be a pleasant surprise in store for us, like finding the nest of a particularly rare breed of duck, or a rat or a weasel held firmly in the jaws of a trap. Cees and I would do our separate rounds of all quarters of the farm and then meet up to compare the various items of news at the end of our tours of inspection. Sometimes a muttered oath from some hedgerow or corner of a pond would intentionally float across from one to the other of us giving advance warning of some catastrophe. For the interchange of good news we both invariably played our cards much closer to our chests.

'Well?' I enquired on the morning of April 21, a day when no *Godverdommens* or other blasphemies had so far disturbed the peace of the farm.

'All is good,' was his non-commital retort, but I detected a slight quivering in his right hand as he struck a match to light his pipe.

'Any excitements?' I persisted, eyeing him carefully.

'Yes.'

At that moment his pipe went out, so there was more fumbling with matches and tobacco, but he looked at me for one brief moment and there was no mistaking the twinkle in his eyes. There was, as he well knew, only one piece of good news that we both wanted to hear, but I just did not dare to put it into words for fear of disappointment. The suspense, however, was unbearable.

'Have we by any chance. . . ?' I left the question uncompleted. Three matches later he was kind enough to nod in the affirmative.

Together and in silence we tiptoed into one of the 'loophole' aviaries and there, in a corner, lay the most beautiful egg that I had ever seen. It was the colour of newly-fallen beech leaves in autumn, heavily blotched with darker chocolate brown.

'Eet looks just like a moorhen egg,' Cees observed with singular irreverence.

During the course of the next four weeks a total of eighteen eggs were laid, all but three of them coming from the birds in the 'loophole' aviaries. Both of these two hens were laying — there was a considerable difference in the shade of brown on the eggs — and on more than one occasion it was clear that they had laid in each others' nests.

After the first six eggs had been laid, we decided to pick them up and hatch them under a broody hen. The rows of scruffy, expressionless Silkies squatting in rows in their nest-boxes, became, second only to the blood pheasants, the objects of our deepest veneration. To one of these was to be entrusted a unique clutch of eggs such as no chicken had ever previously been privileged to sit on. To us it was like selecting the first human being to land on the moon and, had I thought that a diet of Beluga caviar would have assisted the broody in her herculean task, it would have been willingly provided.

Cees and I examined these uninspiring females for over an hour, discussing the respective temperaments and physical attributes of each, but still we could not agree. Cees's choice was one of my original hybrids, a small and hideous female with ingrowing toenails, while my favourite was a two year old pure white Silkie with a light but ample bosom. Eventually, and mindful of the old saying about putting all one's eggs in one basket, we decided on a compromise. Cees's massive fingers slipped three eggs under his beauty queen, while with trembling hands I consigned the same quantity to mine. We had, so the ornithological books told us, twenty-eight days to wait.

Every afternoon punctually at two o'clock all the broodies were taken off their nests for their daily break. For this operation the broody shed was divided into two, Cees dealing with one side and myself with the other, and our two favourites were positioned accordingly. It was an old-fashioned system of hatching, and many modern breeders rely entirely on electrically operated incubators, but it was a method which both of us preferred. Although we had two small incubators constantly running, these were used mainly for the final hatching of waterfowl eggs and as a stand-by against emergencies. The latter were, fortunately, very infrequent, but every year we would have the odd setting ruined by a broody who, without any warning, either started to eat her eggs, or showered them with diarrhoea of elephantine proportions or else expired on her nest.

While the broodies were having their fifteen minute break, Cees and I would go round with two candling lamps. These are simple, hand-made contraptions consisting of an electric light bulb fitted into a biscuit tin with a hole at one end. By holding them to the eggs periodically, we could determine the fertility or otherwise of every egg and check on the proper development of the embryo at its various stages. Fertility can usually be detected by this means after three or four days, but the blood pheasant eggs with their very dark shells rendered inspection much more difficult. It was almost two weeks before we were sure whether they contained any tiny occupants. The score shortly before half-time was: Holland 2, Great Britain 2.

It has been my practice, ever since founding Daw's Hall Wildfowl Farm, to maintain two diaries. One, kept in the foodshed on the farm, has been used by Cees and myself and has been restricted to items of avicultural or farming interest. The entries, such as 'Heel in young sets' or 'Snow due off' are totally unintelligible except to the two of us. Only events of particular importance on the farm are transferred to my house diary, which is intimate, personal and, I hope, equally obscure to outsiders.

The estimated hatching date of our first blood pheasant eggs was transferred somewhat belatedly to the house diary and only then I realized that I was due to dine at the House of Commons on the very evening that the chicks were due to emerge. I do not, I should say, make a practice of having my meals at the power-centre of the nation, but this was an annual reunion dinner of the British officers who had served with the King's African Rifles, and one of our members, a well-known political figure, had generously arranged the venue. Two days before the dinner, there was a tiny chip in two of the four eggs — one to each of us. Cees and I had each agreed to transfer one of our two eggs to an incubator. It was an antediluvian machine, functioning by paraffin, but it had a glass fronted door through which, with the aid of either the candler, or a torch, observation of its hatching-tray was both straightforward and fascinating. At the very moment that I was tying my black tie and preparing to catch a late afternoon train up to London, four little prisoners were struggling to free themselves from their bonds of shell and membrane and break loose into an alien, occidental society.

The dinner seemed to drag on interminably. My own contribution to the general atmosphere of equatorial reminiscenses and back-slapping *bonhomie* was distinctly uninspired. As soon as we had drunk our loyal toast to the Queen, I made a very lame excuse to my neighbour and raced out to hail a taxi. Two hours later and still in evening dress I was crouching on the earth floor of the broody shed, with a torch in one hand and glass of whisky and soda in the other, watching the emergence of our first two chicks. A hurried peep under the two broodies revealed the birth of two more.

The following afternoon, when we moved the babies into two rearing pens with their foster-mothers, we quickly observed how different they were, in both looks and behaviour to any other pheasant chicks that we had seen. Their most striking feature was the vivid vermilion-orange of their beaks, quite different in colour to those of their parents. Other young pheasants are happy to spend most of the first two days of their lives quietly resting under their mothers or close to whatever artificial heat is provided, but these little creatures behaved in a totally original fashion. They were like animated bumble-bees, rushing round their tiny pens at great speed, jumping on and off the backs of their foster-mothers and pecking avidly at the various items on the menu that we had concocted for them.

All the birds at Daw's Hall and particularly the young ones are outrageously spoilt. My accountant tries without much success to draw my attention to this fact every year and I can tell too, from the raised eyebrows of visitors who come at feed time, that our reluctance to subject our menagerie to anything but the best does not go unnoticed. For the blood pheasant chicks, three quarters of the floor space in their brooders was occupied by bowls of assorted delicacies, while in the remaining area available a pampered bantam of dubious ancestry presided over this Indonesian-style banquet. There were tiny millet seeds, finely chopped hardboiled egg, fresh duckweed, chick crumbs garnished with multivitamin powder, shredded leaves of lettuce and dandelion, grated carrot and diminutive mealworms.

One chick succumbed to a surfeit of hardboiled egg and expired from acute constipation on the third day, but the remaining three flourished and made excellent progress. By the sixth day we noticed that two of the chicks had the faintest tinge of blue-grey on their shoulders. These, as we suspected, turned out to be young cocks. It was an intersting observation for, to the best of my knowledge, determination of sex in this way and at this age is not possible with any other species of pheasant.* Each day we moved the brooders onto fresh ground and it was noticeable, when we increased their floor-space, how the chicks avidly plucked the seed heads of various dwarf grasses that came up through the wire mesh flooring.

When they were about a week old, Cees announced that he had found an ants' nest containing masses of eggs under a big stone outside the cottage. We both knew that these eggs have excellent nutritional value, so I told him to add one further dish to the collection and that I would walk round shortly to observe the reaction of the chicks. Their response was instantaneous and highly disconcerting, and it was fortunate that I appeared on the scene very soon after Cees had dispensed the eggs. He had selected a particularly active nest of red ants and had tipped the whole thing, including some of the soldier ants into the two pens. I found the broody hens and chicks leaping frantically in all directions and the banqueting table looked as though it had been subjected to a sudden tornado.

Altogether that year nine blood pheasant chicks were hatched and of these we successfully reared six. Anxious to produce generous dividends to my kind but crazy shareholders, I sold off that autumn several pairs of birds, some young and some wild-caught. By distributing the birds among other pheasant breeders, we hoped not only to minimize the risk of infection, but also that others would be able to experiment with various techniques and add to the very sparse knowledge of these creatures so far available.

*We have since detected minute differences among many other species. It is an interesting subject for further research.

It was, unfortunately, a grave error of judgement. All the birds that we sold died without breeding, and our own stock too began to dwindle. It was soon clear that the problems of maintaining a healthy stock of these particular pheasants in captivity were manifold. Not only were they extremely susceptible to every known avian ailment, and several unknown ones too, but they were also highly accident-prone. The crowning insult occurred when a magnificent young cock, who had an insatiable desire for peanuts, managed somehow to get one stuck in his windpipe and choked to death.

Another little crisis affecting the blood pheasants occurred during the childrens' summer holidays. I was cutting the grass outside the aviaries with a rotary mower and Angus and Katrina were helping by raking up the grass behind me.

'Daddy, why are the blood pheasants running about in the wood?' It was Angus's shrill little voice and my heart missed a couple of beats. I quickly realized, however, that he must be referring to the golden pheasants that were at liberty round the main pond.

'No, darling,' I explained patiently, 'those are the birds that we bought ages ago. Don't you remember how they jumped around in their cardboard boxes all the way home in the car?'

'Sorry, Daddy.'

Ten minutes later it was Katrina's turn to announce: 'Daddy, I saw a bluffezy near the big pond.'

This time I switched off the machine and looked carefully at the aviaries. No doors were open and the catches were all in position. The children and I walked down towards the main pond and there, sure enough, were two blood pheasants happily grazing on the short grass beneath the big cedar. How they had got there I could not for the life of me imagine.

'Told you so, Dad,' echoed the children. '*Kik, keeek, kik, kik,*' came the happy chorus from the bluffezies. It was my turn to apologize.

Cees, as always seemed to happen during moments of dire distress on the farm, was away, this time discussing slug control with a fellow bulbous eccentric. Our normal method of catching pheasants was to pop a trout landing-net over them, a system that was reasonably straightforward in a covered aviary, but the chances of it succeeding in open woodland were obviously remote.

The only faint hope of success that I could see was to walk them back towards their aviary and trust that somehow or other we could induce them to hop back inside. If they were to become alarmed and take to their wings I knew we should never see them again.

We propped the aviary door open, placed some peanuts and hard-boiled egg just inside the entrance and quietly walked round the back of the pond. Then, very slowly, we drove the truant pair back towards their home. When there was only another twenty yards to go, Angus and Katrina went off to the right and left flanks respectively while I continued the main advance on my own. The operation went off without a hitch and within a short while the birds were safely back in their aviary. As I closed the door behind them I saw that a small section of the wire netting had been torn open by the rotary mower passing too close to the front of their pen. It was a very shame-faced Daddy who carried out emergency repairs, before driving down to the local shop to buy double rations of choc-ices for lunch.

Apart from our blood pheasants, the birds that caused us most anguish and frustration were the black swans. The original birds had arrived the year before Cees started work on the farm and they occupied a special pond on the lawn in front of the house. Every morning I shaved and dressed to the accompaniment of their high-pitched, trumpeting calls and my dressing-room window afforded a marvellous view of these stately natives of Australia. By the time they were three years old Cassius and Claudia were clearly ready to breed. Several times I saw Cassius astride his mate, their long black necks extended in parallel, and Claudia's body submerged beneath his in the water. Cassius also became extremely aggressive towards us, and running the gauntlet to top up their food bowl every morning brought back painful memories of Henry, the cereopsis gander. Cees told me that he knew many people in Holland who reared cygnets every year and he told me that breeding pairs almost invariably brought off two clutches, the first in February or March and the second about five months later. We took piles of nesting material — bracken, twigs, grass — into their pen and settled back happily to await the arrival of the first egg. No egg however was forthcoming and it appeared to us that Cassius and Claudia, while perfectly happy to indulge in endless sexual frolics on the water, had no intention of having a family. The only occasion they went near the nest that we had built for them was to chuck the contents into the pond.

One day a Dutch breeder came over to buy a large quantity of waterfowl that we had reared and we took him down to the black swans' enclosure, hoping that he would be able to suggest a solution to our problem. Was it diet, or depth of water, incorrect siting of the nest, or what? For a moment or two he stood regarding our elegant but unproductive pair and then, quite suddenly, he broke into paroxysms of mirth. It was quite some while before he was able to control his laughter and get a word out.

'I theenk your Claudia should be called Claude,' he eventually announced, before doubling up once more.

Later, over lunch, he told us that he thought he could help us resolve the problem of our gay Australians. There were, he explained, a couple of female black swans in a similar predicament in one of the zoos near his home in Holland. These two birds apparently made love as frequently and energetically as ours did, the only difference being that the Dutch couple teamed up periodically on land as well, where they sat side by side on a mammoth nest of infertile eggs.

Within a short while the exchange was effected. Claude flew across the North Sea in a sumptuous wooden crate and two days later the same crate was back at Southend Airport containing Bess. Cassius viewed her arrival with the gravest suspicion. After a brief inspection, he clearly decided that this particular form of second-hand goods was not for him. He sailed majestically to the farthest end of the pool and refused to have anything further to do with her. At the end of Bess's first week at Daw's Hall, Cassius was a different swan. Gone was the aggressive, fighting spirit that he had evinced in protecting his first mate and gone too, was his previous insatiable sexual appetite.

The following year, when both birds had discarded their old feathers and assumed their new breeding plumage, Cees and I decided that the time had come to consider a more ruthless approach to the problem. We summoned the vet, who appeared with a long needle attached to a hypodermic syringe. A liberal dose of hormone injection was pumped into Cassius's left thigh.

'Works all right on cattle and pigs,' said the vet, 'but God knows what effect it will have on this creature.'

The effect was almost instantaneous. Whether from sheer outrage at our ever doubting his sexual prowess, or whether from the drug itself, Cassius quickly resumed his reputation as the fighting Casanova of the farm. Bess was clearly delighted by this sudden change and once again I was able to watch the mating of black swans from my dressing-room window. The new bride, I noticed, was showing a promising little bulge beneath her backside. Fresh nesting material was provided in their pen and hopes once more ran high. These, however, were cruelly dashed when it became all too clear that Cassius was determined on a strict policy of population control. Copulation with Claude, Bess or any further black swans that we might provide for his chauvinistic amusement was one thing, but nest-building and babies were quite definitely not for him. Once again the pond was littered with twigs, bracken and reeds and Bess went into an early moult.

In 1971, as in previous years, we opened the farm to the public every Sunday afternoon in August and September. It was not the favourite occupation of either Cees, Hedy or myself, but it meant a little bit of extra money for all of us and I hoped that the visitors enjoyed themselves. When the final open day of the season arrived I felt only a sense of relief. Another week and I should be on holiday, deer stalking in the north of Scotland. Had anyone suggested that my future wife was to be in one of the parties touring the farm that afternoon, I would in all probability have locked the gate and bolted to Sutherland forthwith. Had Didy's host and hostess given her any inkling of what an innocuous afternoon's outing to visit exotic birds at Daw's Hall Wildfowl Farm would lead to, she would, I suspect, have emigrated for good.

Though we had never previously met, Didy and I had heard of each other through many mutual friends and we had more than one thing in common. Her previous husband had been an officer in my regiment and both our respective marriages had sadly come adrift. When she had arrived at the gate leading into the birds, I myself was down by the island pond with another party and I would not, in all probability have ever been aware of her presence on the farm, had it not been for the fact that neither she nor her friends had any small change with which to buy their admission tickets. I was just embarking on a dreary monologue to my group of visitors on the difficulties of breeding red-breasted geese in captivity, when a kind lady from the village, who was in charge of the till that day, came rushing up to me.

'Have you got change for a tenner?' she asked. 'Some late arrivals want to look round. There's a man, two women and several children. The women have got no money at all and the man has got nothing less than a ten pound note.'

'Bloody plutocrats,' I mumbled. 'What do they think this is, the Royal Enclosure at Ascot?' I should, of course, have been forewarned. Women who are late and carry no money are invariably dangerous.

While this opulent party were leaning nonchalantly against the gate and awaiting the cashier's return, Didy noticed some of my books for sale on a trestle-table. The titles meant nothing to her whatever, but the name of the author clearly rang a bell.

'Oh, God, not *him*,' she was heard to remark.

'Do you know him?' enquired the cashier, who had just returned.

'Well, not really, but I know *of* him,' Didy mumbled, recollecting stories of a retired, divorced Green Jacket officer who spent his time dispensing corn to strange ducks in the wilds of Suffolk. The notice in the local paper, advertising Daw's Hall Wildfowl Farm being open to the public that Sunday, had meant nothing to her at all. It had just been a toss-up between that and Tarzan at the local cinema for keeping her hosts' children amused that afternoon. When the sun came out, Tarzan lost.

'I'll introduce him to you if you like,' said my friendly cashier.

Didy found her tour round the birds quite fascinating. Apart from the waterfowl in St. James's Park and a pair of black swans that she had seen in the Governor's garden in Hong Kong, her previous experience of waterfowl and pheasants had been strictly culinary. The poor cashier-cum-temporary guide was subjected to a barrage of questions, many of which she was quite unable to answer. As they were emerging through the gate at the end of their tour, I was walking across the lawn towards the house. 'Thank goodness, that's over for another year,' I told myself, and promptly turned by thoughts to high tea and a quiet evening reading the Sunday newspapers.

'Iain?' It was the cashier. 'Sorry to bother you, but some visitors here would like to meet you and one lady has got some questions that I'm afraid I can't answer.'

I groaned inwardly. Reluctantly, I turned round and saw some rather smart people admiring the iceberg roses. 'Aha, the ten pound-noters,' I remembered. 'Plenty of change in the house, so I won't let *them* go off without paying.' Aloud, I asked if I could help them.

Much to my surprise, they were perfectly charming and most complimentary about the farm. The questions were shrewd and intelligent and I promptly lowered the drawbridge. 'Why don't you all come in and have some tea?'

The garrulous one, who I had noticed was extremely attractive, accepted with alacrity for all of them.

'No, Didy, we really must get back,' said the man of the party. 'We've got. . .'

'Didy?' I mused. It was an unusual name and I tried hard to think where I had heard it before. Suddenly it came to me. 'You're not Didy Colville by any chance, are you?'

Her smile was utterly captivating. 'Yes, I am. And I know all about *you*.'

'Oh?'

Six weeks later, we were engaged to be married. And I never succeeded in extracting an entrance fee.

Didy's son, Hugh, who was then aged four, was as thrilled with the strange menagerie as was his mother. He formed, too, the firmest of friendships with Angus and Katrina (who were then seven and five) and the three of them spent part of every holidays with us at Daw's Hall.

Didy and I had arranged to get married at the end of August, 1972. But that summer was made particularly hectic by two unforeseen occurrences, the first medical and the second political. Shortly after I had returned from my second expedition to the Himalayas I started to get pain in one of my hips and this had gradually worsened. Both the doctor and the specialist diagnosed osteo-arthritis and the latter said he would be happy to perform an arthroplast any time I felt inclined.

'Arthro- what?' I asked.

'Oh, it just means sawing out your existing hip-joint and inserting an artificial one in its place.'

The whole thing sounded excrutiatingly bloodthirsty, so I politely declined his offer and took aspirins instead. The pain, however, became acute and I had the greatest difficulty in doing any physical work at all on the farm that summer, which meant that Cees and Didy had an extra burden on their shoulders. Didy fortunately took to aviculture like a fish to water, but she, too, was handicapped by still being tied to a job in London for five days every week. She would arrive exhausted at Daw's Hall on a Friday evening just in time to cater for about a thousand avian mouths and usually several human ones as well over the weekend. It was certainly a testing time.

Eventually she dragged me off to see another surgeon, this time in London, and his diagnosis was identical to that of the first man I had seen. Again, the dreaded word arthroplast was mentioned and this time, after he had promised faithfully that I would neither see nor feel anything, I agreed to have the operation. A date in October was fixed, six weeks after we were due to be married.

When there was only a week of my second bachelorhood remaining, an ex-lance corporal of mine, residing in newly acquired splendour thousands of miles away in equatorial Africa, dramatically announced to the world that he was evicting forthwith every Asian from Uganda.

President Idi Amin had been in power for approximately eighteen months. He was a man who combined qualities of leadership and patriotism with an ebullient sense of humour, and he had achieved considerable distinction as a sergeant-major and platoon commander in the King's African Rifles. The natural process of evolution, coupled with his own limited intelligence, should have debarred him from progressing any further. Ignorance among the erstwhile colonial powers, however, had opened the door to inevitable chaos and confusion, not only in Uganda, but in every African territory that had achieved premature independence. Seven years previously I had concluded my book *Jambo Effendi* with the following words:

> "In 1894 *Punch* had published a cartoon of John Bull standing on his doorstep and surveying a black infant, which was lying there, helpless and howling, in a basket labelled 'Uganda'. The captain underneath read 'What, another!! — Well, I suppose I must take it in!!!' The plethora of explanation marks were presumably intended to convey to Victorian readers the humour of the situation. Seventy years had elapsed since then, but the baby still lay there, very much in need of help, howling intermittently, and only the exclamation marks were missing."

Amin, the publicity-mad extrovert, was, by howling the loudest, currently stealing the limelight, but this was just the tip of the iceberg. . .

As one of Amin's closest European friends, I was asked by the British government to fly out to Uganda and endeavour to make him understand that, apart from committing economic suicide, he was hanging a great big label of 'racist' round his own neck. Amin reluctantly agreed to extend the deadline for the Asians' departure from 'forthwith' to 'ninety days,' and I got back to London just in time to change into a clean shirt for our wedding.

This was not the only occasion when I was asked to go and see my erstwhile sergeant-major. Four years later I was one of two envoys who carried a personal letter to Amin from the Queen, when she pleaded for clemency in the case of a British lecturer sentenced to death by firing squad. That, however, is another story. . .

Chapter Eight

Six weeks after being carved up I was back home, hobbling round the farm on crutches. It was November and all the birds were in their newly acquired breeding plumage. For the first time I was able to sit peacefully beside the various ponds and enclosures while everyone else rushed around frantically doing all the work as well as administering to my needs. Early morning tea provided by a devoted wife, enforced afternoon rests and abolition of high tea for more substantial evening repasts were, I decided, a distinct improvement on my previous way of life. It gave me more time to relax and admire the beauty and serenity of our surroundings, and plenty of time, too, to dream up future projects and extensions for the farm. Late autumn, the one time of the year when our income from sales of birds marginally exceeded our expenses, was invariably a period of delightful financial recklessness.

Wild and extravagant plans for stocking the water-meadows with llamas, otters and herds of deer, and opening up a wildlife park were accordingly submitted to the planning authorities. Endless meetings with armies of officials took place, but it was soon apparent that there were several major obstacles in our way. Chief of these was the fact that our meadows on either side of the Stour were about to be designated an area of outstanding natural beauty. Our arguments that a wildlife park would in fact give people, other than casual trespassers, poachers and ourselves, an opportunity actually to see and appreciate the said sacred area were, sadly, not received with any enthusiasm. The gentlemen with bulging briefcases were clearly far more concerned with the problems of traffic congestion and sewage disposal that a wildlife park would create. The local press did not make matters any easier for us by assuming that every wildlife park has to have rampaging herds of elephants, giant boa constrictors and potentially man-eating lions included in its collection. Many of the neighbours viewed our project with considerable alarm and the planners firmly but politely turned down our application.

Cees was most upset by this decision. For months he had been poring over old Dutch manuals, selecting all sorts of exciting animals and birds for us to keep in the park and deciding on the best milk-yielding breeds of goats for the childrens' corner. There was one particular creature that was, I was told, tremendously popular in parks and zoos on the continent, which Cees was determined we should keep, even when he heard that our application had been turned down. It had the unlikely title of the Vietnamese pot-bellied pig.

'They need very leettle space,' he explained, 'And ve could easily keep a few under ze apple trees in ze vegetable garden.'

'All right,' I said without much enthusiasm. 'How do we get hold of a pair?'

Cees had done his homework on the history and current status of pot-bellied pigs in this country. Two hundred years or more ago the first importations of pigs from the East had taken place and systematic selection of breeds had started in Britain. Some of these pigs came from China, where there are more than a hundred known domestic varieties, and others from Indo-China. All these Eastern swine were smaller than the indigenous type and all had one very valuable characteristic. Their early maturity made them particularly easy for the commercial pig-breeders to fatten while young. The Indo-Chinese ones were apparently always black; many had pendulous bellies, and it was through them that the Berkshire pig was developed. The original Chinese and Indo-Chinese strains had become gradually rarer in this country until they disappeared altogether.

In 1959, Whipsnade Zoo arranged for some Vietnamese pot-bellied pigs — a boar and two sows — to be imported from East Berlin Zoo. The three pigs were duly crated and made ready for export, but when the boxes were opened on arrival in this country there were eight pigs inside. Five piglets had been born in transit. Encouraged by this unexpected windfall, which clearly belied the old adage about buying a pig in a poke, Whipsnade set about a further programme of propagation of pot-bellied piglets. More

129

than fifty were reared and dispersed to various zoos and private breeders in this country. The Whipsnade population, however, gradually dwindled and by 1972 there remained one solitary boar. No proper records had been kept of the whereabouts of his pot-bellied kin, nor were any further importations possible, owing to the strict regulations aimed at preventing introduction of foot-and-mouth, rabies and other diseases.

'I haf spoken to the Curator at Whipsnade,' Cees told us, 'and he is happy to give us their boar if only we can find a mate for it.'

Inevitably, for all of us, the tracking down of one of the Whipsnade females or her progeny became an absorbing and important task. Had they all finished up in slaughter-houses? Had they been crossed out of recognition from their pot-bellied, oriental ancestors? Or, as Cees was convinced, was there still a tiny remnant lurking in some remote area of the British Isles? Cees and Hedy suggested that all four of us should go into partnership and that no pigsty should be left unturned until we had resolved the case of the missing sow or sows.

We advertised in the national papers and the farming journals and the response was extraordinary. Nobody actually admitted to owning a pot-bellied pig, but everyone who replied — and they were all owners of zoos or wildlife parks — begged us to put them on top of our list for supplying progeny as soon as we had succeeded in breeding from them. Money, it appeared, was no object. They had seen these creatures on the continent and were well aware of their crowd-drawing properties. Our order book ran to several thousands of pounds, but still there was no trace of the corpulent, dusky lady who would make all this possible.

One day, when Didy and I were out to lunch, a battered Ford van drew up at the farm just as Cees was about to go off to the cottage for his lunch. The driver explained that his widowed mother, who had a passion for old and rare breeds of sheep and pigs, had bought a pair of Vietnamese pigs about ten years previously and had kept them on her smallholding in Yorkshire. Only one litter, totalling seven, had been born and the sow had crushed all but two at birth, The original pair had died, as had the young boar, and all that remained was a five year old gilt.

'Mum saw your advert in t'*Farmer's Weekly* and reckoned as you'd better 'ave t'owd gal.'

He opened the back of the van and there, reclining like a female

Buddha on a pile of fresh straw, was the most gorgeous and desirable female that Cees had ever seen. Twenty minutes later the van headed back to the Yorkshire dales with twelve Silkie pullets in the back and two ten pound notes in the driver's pocket. When we got back from our lunch party, I saw that there were a couple of sheep hurdles across the entrance to the garage. Cees was leaning on these, a huge cigar in his mouth, lovingly scratching the back of the object of our dreams.

Sache, our pot-bellied sow, arrived in style.

I telephoned Whipsnade straight away. How soon could they send up the boar? It was, they explained, a very busy time of the year: a lot of the staff were away on holiday, but they were coming up to Colchester Zoo to collect some animals in six weeks time and would bring the boar to us then. Didy went off to the local miller's to get a few bags of feed while I looked up my old Cirencester notes on the daily ration of meal for a sow. Sache (which is Dutch for Sarah) settled down happily in her new surroundings and clearly adored human company. The children spent part of the Easter holidays with us and every morning after breakfast the three of them would climb over the gate and give her various scraps from the kitchen. She was the most docile and friendly creature imaginable, and Angus, Katrina and Hugh spent hours scratching her behind the ear as she lay with a rapturous expression on her face and her huge belly heaving with contentment.

After a couple of weeks Cees told me that he was worried that Sache was putting on too much weight. None of us had had any previous experience of keeping pigs so our animal husbandry was very much a matter of guesswork. He and I agreed, however, that perhaps we were overfeeding her and that her daily ration should be reduced by a third. With the children back at school, we knew that a closer check on her diet could be maintained and that, until the summer holidays, there would be no further packets of cereal or loaves of bread disappearing mysteriously from the kitchen. Despite the reduction in her daily feed, Sache's figure still continued to increase in size. About a week later, while they were leaning over the gate of the makeshift pigsty discussing the problem, Didy and Cees saw her pushing all the straw into a corner. She was showing obvious symptoms of restlessness and discomfort. Cees climbed into the pen and gently squeezed her teats. Drops of milk fell onto the straw.

Cees had been far too excited at her arrival three weeks previously to think of writing down the name and address of her erstwhile owners. All we knew for certain was that she was born somewhere in Yorkshire, that her brother had died from some obscure complaint shortly before she had come to us and that the previous owners had a delapidated Ford van. We could only assume that she had been served by her brother before he died. Cees assured us that he would know, as soon as the piglets were born, if their sire was anything but a pure Vietnamese boar.

That afternoon we took one of the duck-rearing lamps from the farm and hung it over Sache's bed. As soon as Cees had checked that what he always called the 'thrommometer' was giving a suitable reading, I went off and telephoned the vet to get his advice over the construction of a farrowing crate. We certainly wanted no repetition of any accidents such as had befallen most of Sache's own brothers and sisters. I was writing down the dimensions when Cees burst into the study, showering mud from his size sixteen gumboots all over the carpet.

'Come quick!' he shouted. 'She harrows. . . it is treeplets!'

'Farrowing, not harrowing, you great clot,' I laughed, as we rushed together to the garage. By the time we got there the triplets had become quadruplets and we wondered whether more were to come. Sache looked up proudly but wearily in our direction before sinking back with a great sigh of contentment into the straw. We agreed that all we could do was to leave her in peace and hope for the best. We had one final peep through a crack in the door, but, although there were little squeaks from within, her broad backside was towards us and there was no way of counting piglets without disturbing her.

The following morning we woke around five o'clock. Further sleep was impossible, so Didy and I donned dressing-gowns and slippers and tiptoed towards the garage door. From within came the sound of human voices. Cees and Hedy, similarly attired, had beaten us to it. 'One male, three females,' Cees announced proudly. 'And I'm sure they're pure Vietnamese pot-bellies.'

Sache proved to be an admirable mother and the little piglets grew at a splendid rate. There was no mistaking their breed: apart from their enchanting snub noses, wicked little eyes and diminutive legs, they seemed to be almost all belly. When the weather became warmer and the piglets were about a month old, we decided to give them more fresh air and exercise. Cees put up some sheep netting round the apple trees in the vegetable garden and converted an old chicken arc into sleeping quarters for the family. They were happily installed when the Whipsnade boar arrived. The Curator, who came with him, was somewhat perplexed by the fact that our breeding programme had already got under way, and we agreed that as soon as Sache's first litter had been weaned we should put her to the Whipsnade boar for we were anxious to introduce a new blood line.

Cees christened the boar Cobus — 'it's Dutch for dirty old man,' he explained — and put him in the garage recently vacated by Sache and her litter. Ponderous, lethargic and covered in warts, Cobus had, we understood, never seen a female of his species for eight of his nine years, and it seemed to us highly unlikely that he could live up to his name.

Meanwhile Sache and her family were having a blissfully happy time rootling around in their new enclosure. One Saturday morning, while we were having breakfast, they rootled rather too hard. Sache managed to lift the bottom of the wire netting with her snout and the four little piglets had wriggled out. Our first intimation of trouble was when we heard Sache screaming lustily as she tried unsuccessfully to follow them. Abandoning our kippers, we rushed outside to hear a joyful squealing from the flower-beds and to see devastation among the dahlias. Surprised in the act, the piglets bolted, literally *ventre à terre*, past Cees's cottage, fortunately avoiding his fritillaries, and down the lane towards the river, bristles erect and tails rampant like warthogs.

Cees, hearing the hullabaloo, soon joined us and we were working out a plan of action when the unmistakable sound of a hunting horn floated down the valley towards us. Looking to our right we saw pink coats and horses approaching at some speed.

As the only member of the party unable to run, I hobbled back towards the road to act as long-stop if the piglets decided to change course and take on the weekend traffic. I also hoped from the high ground to be able to signal to the hunt. Cees set to work on erecting a trapping area in a corner of the vegetable garden, while Didy went off towards the river to drive the piglets back towards their mother. As she got to within sight of the Stour, an ashen-faced fisherman came rushing up the lane towards her. 'W-w-wild boar,' he stammered as he bolted for the safety of his car. With some difficulty Didy managed to restrain him and explain what had happened. He had been quietly enoying his sport on the river's bank when he had heard a rustling noise just behind him. Turning round, he had come face to face with four wicked little black snouts and eight beady eyes inches away from his ground bait.

Didy, assisted by the fisherman, who was now intrigued by the incident and also anxious to retrieve his rod and tackle bag that had been abandoned in his flight, succeeded in rounding up the truant piglets and they were safely driven into Cees's catching area

'Wild boar' sent a fisherman flying for the safety of his car.

just as the leading hounds were beginning to pick up the scent. That day we invested in a roll of electric fencing.

When the piglets were nine weeks old we presented a pair to Whipsnade and left Alice and Puck, the two remaining girls, to amuse themselves in the vegetable garden. A reluctant Sache was frog-marched back to the garage to join her prospective bridegroom. Cobus's reaction was one of utter terror. He cowered in the corner and buried his ugly old head in the straw every time Sache came anywhere near him. It was an unpropitious start to the honeymoon. When Cees fed them every morning and evening, Sache did her best to eat her reluctant spouse's food as well as her own, so Cees had to give him a separate trough and stand guard over it until he had had his fill. Sache for her part became increasingly unpleasant towards Cobus and we decided that the only thing to do was to separate them until she came on heat.

A week or so later, when Didy and I had been up to London for the day, we got back to find the van of the local hunt parked right outside the garage. After the earlier incident with the hounds, we wondered what new crisis had occurred. However, when we saw Cees and the driver amicably leaning over the hurdles and chatting unconcernedly, our fears subsided.

'All well?' I asked.

Cees looked at us quizzically for a moment or two while fumbling for the inevitable pipe and matches. The back of the van was open and, glancing inside, I saw lying on the floor the corpse of poor Cobus. His head was turned towards me and I remember thinking that it was the only time I had ever seen him looking happy.

'Poor old Cobus, what on earth's happened to him?' Didy asked.

'Sache came on heat this morning,' Cees explained, 'so I open up ze gate between them and stand here vatching just like this to see that all is vell. Cobus he sniff around for a few minutes and then he try to climb onto her back. Poor old boy, I theenk he was out of practice...'

'And what happened?'

'Vell, after a little while I see him frothing at the mouth and then he made an enormous effort and he mounted onto her back and serviced her very good.'

'Served,' I corrected.

'Ach so, served. Then, just as he was finished, woomf! I theenk he have a heart-attack because he fall down stone-dead. So I telephone the hunt for them to collect the body for the hounds.' Cees paused for a moment, drew on his pipe and a wondrous expression came over his face. 'Godverdommen, vat a vay to go!'

Cobus's final few minutes on this earth had not been wasted. Three months later it was clear that Sache was once again in pig. What had not occurred to us, however, was that the frolicking of her first litter in the vegetable garden had been something rather more than innocent porcine games. Cees was the first to realize that the distorted and pendulous bellies of Alice and Puck could not be entirely attributed to their breed. We were now in imminent danger of a population explosion of pot-bellied pigs without having any proper pigsty or farrowing quarters. All but one of the pig-lamps were in use for the young waterfowl and pheasants, however the electrician in Sudbury had just two more in stock which we quickly acquired. Puck was brought in to Cobus's old pen next to her mother, while a tiny shed on the farm was converted into a place for Alice's confinement. The two gilts gave birth to four apiece without trouble, but the arrival of the offspring of Sache and the late-lamented Cobus was far more dramatic.

Cees had carefully worked out when she was due to farrow, and it was about a week before this date that Didy and I went out to dinner with some friends who lived nearby. I remember thinking as we got into the car that I must remind Cees to rig up Sache's lamp and give her fresh straw the next day. At one o'clock in the morning, as I was parking the car outside the garage, I heard little squealing noises from within. It did not sound like Puck's babies, who were then a fortnight old, so I opened the door and switched on the light. There were newly-born piglets all over the floor in Sache's pen. A quick count revealed eleven. While Didy, clutching her long dress, carefully stepped over the recumbent form of Sache to put down fresh straw for their bedding, I jumped back into the car and tore down the lane to the cottage. A few blasts on the horn brought a sleepy Cees and Hedy to the window, and minutes later Cees was fixing the pig-lamp in position and we were counting heads. Cobus, we felt, must surely have been grinning happily from his heavenly abode as we joyfully reached a total of fourteen.

Back in the house we opened a bottle of champagne. 'Darling, its no use us ever having a baby,' Didy lamented. 'I know it couldn't possibly give you as much pleasure as having fourteen piglets in one night.'

The fecundity of our pigs that year seemed to have inspired the other inmates on the farm. Cees, Didy and I had a particularly busy summer. There is no doubt that Didy's energy and enthusiasm contributed considerably to this success. Her female intuition and expertise with the rearing of some of the young pheasants was remarkable. The common species of ornamental pheasants, with which we had started and which we found to be almost as easy as chickens to hatch and rear, had gradually been upstaged by an ever increasing number of more difficult species. Lady Amhersts, silvers and red junglefowl joined our peafowl and golden pheasants in the wood round the main pond, while firebacks, white eared and peacock pheasants took over their aviaries. The last named are small, dainty and exquisitely beautiful birds that come from the tropical and sub-tropical jungles of south-eastern Asia. Comparatively little is still known of the life habits of the six different species. They are shy and secretive birds and few people have been fortunate enough to observe them in their natural habitat. To aviculturists they present a real challenge and only a very small number had previously been bred in this country. Although they can be induced to lay several clutches each spring, each clutch contains only one or two eggs, so there is little or no margin for error.

Young peacock pheasant chicks take their food (chiefly live insects) from their mother's bill for the first few days after hatching. Rather remarkably, a few of our broody hens got the knack of feeding these special creatures, but the majority merely scratched the food all over the floor with a look as if to say: 'There you are, help yourselves!' These broodies had to be returned to the hen house and we were forced to resort to artificial rearing of the chicks. An infra-red lamp supplied the heat, but inducing the babies to start feeding was a time-consuming and difficult task.

That year our only pair of Palawan peacock pheasants laid a total of eight eggs, and from these the seven chicks that hatched were all successfully reared. Didy's technique consisted of deft use of a pair of chopsticks — not inappropriate, since this endangered species is confined to the Island of Palawan in the Philippines — with which she spent hours dangling succulent, tiny mealworms in front of their little beaks. Another method of preparing food which she patented was for hard-boiled eggs. These are not only high in protein (an excellent stimulant to breeding birds), but the colour and taste also attract the attention of young waterfowl and pheasants. Cees and I had used hard-boiled eggs for several years, crushing the eggs in our horny hands or laboriously chopping them into fine pieces with a penknife. Whichever system we adopted, many of the adult cock pheasants were quick to recognize the gastronomic relationship between what we provided and what their own hens laid. At one stage egg-eating got so bad in certain pens that it was not uncommon to see a male bird waiting inches away from his wife's posterior, for a succulent egg to emerge.

Didy's method of preparing the hard-boiled egg was to pop the whole thing into her electric mincer. What came out the other end was ground shell, yoke and white of egg, all bound together in pelleted form and in no way resembling the original article.

The mealworms were not only given to young peacock pheasants, but were part of the normal diet of several species of adult and young pheasants. Certain firms specialize in breeding myriads of maggots, mealworms and other creepy-crawlies and despatching them to customers by passenger train or post. For some considerable time we had availed ourselves of this service. Every week during the breeding season the postman had gingerly conveyed to the house a box of wriggling insects and every month I had made out an enormous cheque to the firm concerned. Didy's frugality and commonsense saw this as an unnecessary extravagance with the amount we were using, so we decided to breed our own live insect food. Mealworms, which are the larval stage of a beetle that feeds on bran or flour, are, so the pamphlet told us, easily propagated all year round, so long as they can be kept in a warm, dark area.

Didy, having suggested the idea, was put in charge of the operation, which was not without its teething problems. At first it seemed as if we had been landed with a carnivorous strain of beetle, since no sooner had the eggs hatched into writhing masses of tiny mealworms than they all suddenly disappeared.

'I'm sure its due to overcrowding,' explained the mealworm queen. 'You'll have to buy me a lot more fish tanks.'

I had only just been handed the bill for the first fish tank and it was not difficult to calculate that the cost of three or four more of these, together with the running expenses of the heating lamp which would have to be suspended over them, was going to add up to an enterprise that would score nought out of ten for cost effectiveness.

In an attempt to economize, we bought cheap plastic containers and placed these close to an existing source of heat — the radiator in the childrens' playroom. During their first night in these new premises scores of mealworms and beetles escaped and Hugh, Katrina and Angus spent the following morning retrieving them from every conceivable crevice and cranny in the house.

I was despatched to the local ironmonger for further capital expenditure — this time fly-proof zinc gauze.

The next problem came when we discovered that a lot of beetles were dying for no apparent reason.

'Old age,' suggested Angus.

139

'Lack of moisture,' contradicted Didy, who sent Angus and me off to the chemist, this time to buy glass test-tubes.

These were filled with water and placed in one corner of each container with a wad of cotton wool to prevent the occupants from drowning. Several unfortunate beetles and mealworms, desperate to slake their thirst, succeeded in burrowing through the cotton wool and met a watery grave.

Cees finally came to the rescue. 'I theenk ze vorms like apples,' he said

The test tubes were removed and the children cut up apples and oranges, carrots and potatoes, and put these in the bran in each container. It was not long before Didy proudly carried out to the farm her first crop of mealworms for the birds. All went well and further live harvests were garnered and placed in the refrigerator in the kitchen. There, not surprisingly, the cold atmosphere immediately halted both the growth and the appetite of the worms, but taking them out into a warm room or onto the farm gave them a few, final moments of happy wriggling before being devoured by the pheasants.

Early in April, when the weather got warmer, I switched off the central heating. The mealworms, needless to say, did not take kindly to cool days and colder nights. Though they remained alive, they were noticeably less active and the beetles registered their discontent by declining to breed. A lot of the early eggs on the farm were about to hatch and very soon we would be needing maximum output from the playroom.

'You'll have to keep their radiator going till the end of the breeding season,' was the mealworm queen's ultimatum.

'If you think I'm going to run the central heating throughout the summer, just to stimulate the sexual instincts of your beetles, you'd better think again,' I retorted. We looked at each other and laughed.

That evening, when I was getting some clean clothes out of the airing cupboard in the nursery bathroom, I realized that I was looking at the perfect mealworm propagation centre. Sheets and towels, shirts and nether garments were promptly stacked in the farthest corner, and the main part of the shelves was made over to Didy's mealworms. There they instantly showed their appreciation by indulging in an intense programme of procreation, and there doubtless they will remain until the day comes when I find mealworms crawling through my underpants.

Our discovery of the airing cupboard as being the one place where there was permanent warmth and darkness soon led to further experiments in propagation in the nursery bathroom. This time it was sprouting millet and oats. We had for some time been concerned about the best form of green food to supply to the blood pheasants. That they were primarily vegetarian we already knew, but we were extremely conscious of the health hazard both from grass and from lettuce and fruit that might either contain harmful parasites or have been subjected to toxic sprays. Cees and I had often discussed possible green foods that could be grown in a totally sterile environment and now we realized that the airing cupboard was the answer to our prayers. Once a week Cees, in his size sixteen gumboots, would trapes along the corridor and mount the back staircase, leaving a trail of mud and dripping sand, as he carried tiers of seed-boxes containing millet and oats seed up to the shelf below Didy's mealworms. By sealing each tray in a black polythene bag, the seeds in their damp bed of sand quickly germinated and after six or seven days were about two inches high and ready for avian consumption. The fine shoots from the millet seed were, we found, ideal for the young blood pheasants, of which we reared two that year.

The airing cupboard became an increasingly popular haunt and on one night it gave warmth and shelter to an abandoned pot-bellied piglet. Alice had, needless to say, farrowed at a thoroughly inconvenient time: we had far too many Vietnamese piglets for the limited accommodation available, and Didy and I were due to go off to Jersey for a week the following day. There were several reasons for this visit to the Channel Islands. The first operation on my hip-joint had not been a complete success and I had recently been carved up again. The surgeon had prescribed post-operative peace and quiet and plenty of swimming, and it was a good excuse to stay in a hotel that had a heated swimming pool. (Power cuts from industrial strife in England had ruled out all hotels on the mainland!) The other motives were even less altruistic: scrumptious sea-food, cheap drink and the close proximity of Gerald Durrell's Jersey Wildlife Preservation Trust. Previous visits to the latter had not only given us enormous pleasure, but enabled us to meet a dedicated group of people who shared our own philosophy on proper management of endangered creatures in captivity.

The unfortunate piglet could not have arrived on the scene at a worse moment. Alice had eaten all its brothers and sisters at birth and had denied milk to the sole survivor. Cees rescued it from certain death and it had, remarkably, survived a night in the airing cupboard, surrounded by sprouting oats and copulating beetles. If it was to have any hope of remaining alive, intensive care for the next few days was essential. It was desperately weak.

Didy didn't hesitate. 'I'll take it to Jersey with us,' she announced and promptly went off in the car to Sudbury to buy bottles, teats and dried milk.

While she was administering the first feed in the kitchen, I hobbled in on my crutches and suggested that there might possibly be certain health restrictions regarding the importation of cloven-footed animals to the Channel Islands.

'Don't be silly, darling,' she replied. 'Piggy is not being imported or exported, and he certainly won't be coming into contact with any other cloven-hoofed animals. All he needs is a tourist visa. I'm sure the hotel won't mind.' She turned her attention back to the kettle of boiling water, sterilising equipment and one of our best towels from which a little pink snout emerged.

'No, I'm sure they won't,' I replied wearily. 'They probably have special rates for orphaned piglets.'

Piggy duly arrived at Southend Airport in Didy's Carmen roller bag, with the rest of his requirements carefully packed in her overnight case. Just as we stepped into the airport building there was a peal of thunder and the heavens opened. Having booked in for the flight, Didy retired to the ladies cloakroom where she locked herself in the lavatory and gave him his next feed. Temporarily fortified, he was beginning to exercise his vocal chords and Didy found a very startled attendant regarding her when she eventually emerged from the closet.

An announcement came over the public address system. Owing to bad weather conditions our flight to Jersey was to be delayed for at least an hour. We sat in the airport lounge reading our newspapers, the Carmen roller bag on Didy's lap, with a crack open for ventilation. After half an hour instinct told her that all was not well and she gingerly opened the bag and put her hand inside.

'Piggy's dead,' she said quietly.

In the circumstances it was, perhaps, just as well.

Chapter Nine

For the thirteen years that Daw's Hall Wildfowl Farm has been in existence it has always been my conviction that the main criterion for keeping birds and animals in captivity is the establishment of optimum breeding facilities. The rarer the creature, the more important this is. Over the last decade the necessity for conservation has, belatedly, begun to take root in peoples' minds and there is a growing awareness of our responsibility towards the constantly threatened balance of plants and animals on the earth's surface. Zoos, wildlife parks and smaller collections all have an important role in helping to maintain viable breeding stocks of endangered species for posterity to see and to study. Some of these establishments, through the farsightedness of their management and dedication of their staff, have made and continue to make important contributions to conservation; others, sad to relate, have not.

Bad husbandry, exploitation and often criminal ignorance lie behind a veneer of laughing chimpanzees, gaudy macaws and strutting peacocks. Lax legislation in many countries is partly to blame. Even in England I am amazed that I need no licence to keep what is now one of the largest collections of endangered pheasants and waterfowl in existence. Officials descend on the farm periodically to examine our forestry plantations and to check our electricity and water consumption, but nobody from the Ministry has ever called to enquire whether I innoculate my pheasants and poultry against fowl pest, or whether I use my stock for taxidermy.

The hackneyed words of the old song *Money is the root of all Evil* are unpalatable but true. In the field of wildlife preservation they apply all too often, and the search for rare creatures frequently encourages abuse of the ethics of conservation. The giant panda, symbol of the World Wildlife Fund and darling of the journalists, has often been assumed to be in a state of permanent persecution in its native China. Despite our cuddly toys and occidental sentimentality, it was from the West that serious harassment of the panda originated. The first specimen to be shot by a westerner was collected by the Roosevelts in 1929. The display of this skin in the Chicago Natural History Museum, together with a live specimen secured by the Chicago Zoo a few years later, resulted in a mad stampede by other museums and zoos to collect specimens. This, so far as is known, is the only period in the animal's history in which it has been seriously threatened with extinction.

The collection of certain birds and animals for protected breeding away from threatened areas is becoming increasingly important as a method of saving species whose numbers have become dangerously depleted in the wild. When properly co-ordinated, it is also a viable means of conducting research into many biological and behavioural factors that will infuence their survival in their countries of origin. This has to be properly controlled on an international basis, and at the same time conservation organizations and governments, particularly in the developing countries, must unite to educate people to a deeper realization of the natural resources upon which, in the final analysis, their own survival depends. Man can no longer afford to assume that nature exists for his convenience.

With our own strange menagerie, on the borders of Suffolk and Essex, it is only fair to admit that our zeal and technical expertise have frequently not matched up to our ideals. Our so-called breeding pair of black swans was a typical example. By the end of 1974 Cassius, accompanied originally by Claudia-or-Claude and latterly by Bess, had been in residence on the farm for more than seven years, and everyone who came to view the collection remarked on his outstanding physique and good looks. 'Where do they nest?' I would be asked, and would then shamefully have to admit that it was one species with which we had had total failure. It was, I would hasten to explain, not from lack of trying. We experimented with different diets, we deepened their pond, we enlarged their territory, but all to no avail. Our lack of success became increasingly painful to me as each year went by, and every time I visited another collection, there would be black swans sitting on eggs or surrounded by adorable cygnets. On one particularly galling occasion Didy and I saw a female squatting contentedly on a great pile of twigs and dried grass only a few feet from a busy main road in France.

It was our Dutch friends, who had so kindly arranged for the earlier exchange, who once again offered to help. In their collection close to the Belgian border was an adult pair which they proposed to sell us. The cock bird, or cob, was apparently a timid and hen-pecked creature, who had so far displayed no symptoms of virility, but the pen was a prolific layer who churned out eggs like a battery hen. This dominant female, we all agreed, was likely to prove the perfect mate for the irascible and libidinous Cassius.

When Cees and I released Porgy and Portia from their crate, we saw them properly for the first time, and were not surprised that there had been no issue from the marriage. She was a good-looking and buxom female, but poor Porgy was nothing but skin and bone. After we had caught up Bess, her successor was launched onto the water in the smart swan enclosure in front of the house. Cassius came scurrying over the water to greet her and they were soon swimming around happily together. There were no such luxurious quarters for the remaining pair. The only spare waterfowl enclosure was a tiny area, shorn of all grass, at the top of one of the streams. It had originally been constructed for two pairs of rare South American teal, but neither they nor any other ducks had ever bred in the cramped surroundings. We put some worming powder and a liberal supply of kibbled maize in a trough of water and hoped that poor, emaciated Porgy would put on a bit of weight. It was my intention to sell this pair as soon as possible, but I could not possibly expect any customer to take him in his present condition. The only encouraging factor was that Bess, unlike his previous wife, did not bully him.

Two days after their arrival a huge lorry drove up to the back door. It belonged to a firm of water engineers who had contracted to sink a trial borehole on the farm. It had long been my intention to increase the flow of water through the series of streams and ponds that we had constructed. A strong and permanent supply of pure water would greatly improve the overall conditions and reduce the risk of disease, and it would enable us to keep goldeneye, smew, mergansers and a host of other rare and exciting waterfowl. We had been warned that sinking the shaft would be a noisy and disruptive business, so it had been agreed that all the work would be completed by the middle of February so that peace would be restored to the farm before the start of the breeding season.

The engineers, Cees and I had already worked out the most likely site for a borehole, which was exactly two yards outside the enclosure of poor Porgy and Bess. So now all the heavy machinery and other paraphernalia was conveyed to this spot. The whole area soon resembled a miniature North Sea oil rig and the noise, as a two-ton mechanical sledgehammer descended every few seconds onto a series of huge steel tubes, was deafening beyond belief. The black swans retreated to the furthest corner of their pen, where a large clump of pampas grass gave them a modicum of seclusion, until four o'clock every afternoon when the men downed tools.

About two weeks later, when Cees and I were discussing with the foreman how much deeper he would have to go before there was a likelihood of finding water, we noticed that the black swans' attraction to the pampas grass was not entirely attributable to its properties as a hiding-place. The two birds were plucking long strands from the clump and passing them over their shoulders onto a neat pile behind them. Bess's backside was duly subjected to scrutiny from where we stood, and we both agreed that there was an optimistic bulge. Cees collected a wheelbarrow full of assorted twigs, leaves and dried grass and dumped these beside the pampas grass. The next day there was no mistaking their intentions. Both the bulge and the nest had increased in size and two days later Bess laid her first egg. Thereafter one of them remained permanently on the nest, while the other continued to pass extra nesting material to its mate. Porgy, fortified by maize and obviously very much in love with his new wife, was a model prospective father, taking long turns to help incubate the five pale green eggs and jealously guarding the nest while his mate was sitting.

Even after the engineers struck water the noise and commotion continued. Plumbers and electricians came, the gantry was dismantled and a pump lowered down the shaft. Porgy and Bess seemed indifferent to all that was going on around them.

In the excitement caused by the discovery and organization of the new supply of crystal-clear water that rushed from pond to pond, to say nothing of the unexpected developments in the tiny enclosure beside the borehole, we had rather forgotten our leading pair of Australian swans. We were caught completely by surprise when one morning I discovered an egg lying close to the water's edge in their pen. Another barrow-load of nesting material was rushed to the site and Cassius belaboured us lustily round the knees with his wing while this instant nest was being created. The moment it was completed and the egg placed on top, Portia climbed into position.

It was interesting to observe the different attitudes to impending parenthood displayed by the two pairs. None of us could imagine the headstrong and foul-tempered Cassius incubating any of their five eggs and to begin with Portia, obviously sharing our doubts as to her spouse's ability to sit still for more than two minutes, remained permanently on the nest herself. One morning hunger and thirst must have driven her to leave the nest and we saw Cassius sitting in her place. As soon as he saw us approach, however, he was on his feet, glaring menacingly towards us, his feathers quivering with anger. Then, suddenly remembering his new role, he slowly and reluctantly subsided back onto the nest. Portia, who had been watching his reactions carefully while endeavouring to have a quick breakfast of grass, grunted with obvious relief. We took a few more paces towards the gate leading into their pen and this time it was too much for him. He rushed off the nest with a loud trumpeting call and charged towards us. Portia immediately took over incubation duty and thereafter we never saw her off the nest for more than ten minutes at a stretch.

Despite the differing characters of our black quartet, the eggs were well tended. The pair by the borehole scored five out of five, while, due perhaps to a slight lapse in Cassius's concentration, he and Portia dropped just one point. The rearing of the nine greyish-white cygnets was admirably carried out by their respective parents. Porgy and Bess, not content with one family, started to nest again when their first cygnets were half grown and able to fend for themselves. In order to give their parents a little more peace and freedom, we removed the five youngsters to a large concrete pond at the other end of the farm, where a very maternal, free-winged barnacle gander flew into their pen and adopted them. This barnacle in fact had a busy season, completing the rearing of no less than three different families, totalling thirteen cygnets in all.

It is experiences such as those we have had with the black swans that bring home all too clearly how much I have still to learn in my chosen career with birds and animals. Even our recent success with this species has left many questions unanswered. There will always be gaps in our knowledge, but it is in the excitement of new discovery that lies one of the fascinations of wildlife. Although all of us who are fortunate enough to be able to keep rare creatures in captivity have a moral obligation to provide to the best of our ability for their welfare, there are times, I believe, when we should accept that nature is the final arbiter and be thankful for the inspiration that it gives to us.